ENVIRONMENTAL MANAGEMENT FOR RURAL TOURISM AND RECREATION

Also available from Cassell:

Aronsson: *The Development of Sustainable Tourism*
Boella and Pannett: *Principles of Hospitality Law*, 2nd Edition
Godfrey and Clarke: *The Tourism Development Handbook*
Hudson: *Snow Business*
Johns and Lee-Ross: *Research Methods in Service Industry Management*
Leask and Yeoman (eds): *Heritage Visitor Attractions*
Lee-Ross (ed.): *HRM in Tourism and Hospitality*
O'Connor: *Using Computers in Hospitality*, 2nd Edition
Ryan (ed.): *The Tourist Experience*
Thomas (ed.): *The Management of Small Tourism and Hospitality Firms*
Webster: *Environmental Management in Hospitality*

Environmental Management for Rural Tourism and Recreation

John  Xavier Font,
Nigel Griffiths, Richard Vickery
and

CASSELL
London and New York

Cassell

Wellington House
125 Strand
London WC2R 0BB

370 Lexington Avenue
New York
NY 10017-6550

First published 2000

British Library Cataloguing-in-Publication Data
A catalogue record for this book is available from the British Library.

ISBN 0-304-70693-0 (paperback)

Typeset by Kenneth Burnley, Wirral, Cheshire.
Printed and bound in Great Britain by Redwood Books, Trowbridge, Wiltshire.

Contents

Acknowledgements

This book has been produced as part of a project – TOURFOR – co-funded by the European Commission (under the LIFE programme of DGXI), Buckinghamshire Chilterns University College (UK), North Karelia Polytechnic (Finland) and Estacão Florestal Nacional (Portugal). We would like to thank these organizations for their generous support.

In the UK, at Buckinghamshire Chilterns University College, we would like also to thank the Director, Professor Bryan Mogford, and the Dean of the Faculty of Leisure and Tourism, Gill Fisher, for their continued encouragement for the project. Additionally, Martin Hamer was instrumental in orchestrating the multidisciplinary aspects of the project, along with Dorette Biggs, Florin Ioras and Trevor Dixon. The UK team have also benefited from much help, comment and insight from practitioners in the field: Richard Broadhurst and Paddy Harrop (Forestry Commission), Barry Collins (Center Parcs), Chris and Anne Yarrow (Wilderness Wood), Andy Barnard (Burnham Beeches), Nigel Tansley Thomas (Foundation for Environmental Education in Europe), David Russell (National Trust), Derek Stickler and Steve Searle (The Crown Estate, Windsor), Richard Williamson (Buccleuch Countryside Service), Sarah Leberman (Massey University, Australia), Mike Ibbitson (CEAC), Marion Lyon (BCTV) and Graham Hunt (Forest of Mercia).

Our sincere thanks also go to our European partners who have worked with us on this book. The Finnish team comprised Raimo Hulmi, Esa Etelätalo, Jussi Somerpalo and Hanna Turunen from North Karelia Polytechnic, with contributions from Lasse Lovén of the Finnish Forest Research Institute. The team from Portugal comprised Professor Francisco Castro Rego, Maria João Jesus and Elsa Teles Silva from Estacão Florestal Nacional. Contributions from the field in Portugal were gratefully received from Ricardo Paiva and Mestre Ribeiro (Tapada Nacional de Mafra), Ana Loureiro and Paulo Lopes (Parque Ecológico de Monsanto), Susana Abrantes and Ana Paula Rodrigues (ICN, Parque Natural de Montesinho), Manuela Direito (ICN, Delegação Regional de Coimbra), Cristina Machado (ICN, Parque Nacional da Peneda – Gerês) and António Relvão.

Finally we would like to acknowledge the encouragement and contribution of David Barker from Cassell in publishing the book, and Yumi Shimizu, a former student at BCUC, who designed the project logo.

John Tribe, Xavier Font, Nigel Griffiths, Richard Vickery and Karen Yale
High Wycombe, January 2000

Introduction

The countryside is the setting where many types of tourism and outdoor recreation take place. A high-quality natural environment is essential for most of these activities: without it they would find it hard to function and many could cease to exist. The last three decades have seen a dramatic growth of participation in outdoor recreation and tourism activities. This has resulted in a large increase in the volume of people demanding access to the countryside and placed considerable pressure on the environment.

For some countryside sites, tourism and recreation are not appropriate activities, perhaps because of the special sensitivity of a site or indeed because of hazards arising from agricultural uses. Elsewhere, tourism may sometimes threaten sustainability of the countryside and its local environment: but it also has the power to support it.

With a positive approach to tourism and recreation management, a harmonious relationship between the visitors and the environment can be formed. If managed carefully, tourism and recreation can help to maintain the environment, rather than inflict damage on it. There exists a relationship of mutual interdependence between tourism, recreation and the countryside environment: they increasingly rely upon each, and because of this, management is important.

The Environmental Management System (EMS) which is the centre of this manual, develops guidelines for environmental management which recognize such interdependence. It seeks to reduce conflict between tourism, recreation and the countryside environment and create a symbiotic relationship, as outlined in the diagram overleaf.

It seeks to encourage countryside tourism and recreation, which is managed to maximize the benefits and minimize the costs to the environment in which it takes place. Benefits can include contribution to the viability of local economies and provision of support for environmentally sound agricultural production. Negative environmental impacts to be minimized include overcrowding, diminution of aesthetic appeal, loss of tranquillity, destruction of natural features, loss of biodiversity, overuse of resources and production of waste products.

This countryside EMS is a response to Agenda 21, an action plan resulting from the 1992 Earth Summit, aimed at environmental improvement at the corporate level.

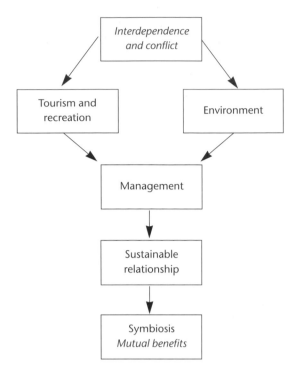

It uses the EMS approach to implant sustainable aims into organizational missions and encourage systematic delivery of sustainable practices. It has unique features including:

- development in partnership with EU countries;
- compatibility with other management systems and has partial compatibility with EMAS and ISO 14000 approaches;
- emphasis on locally set agendas for environmental improvement;
- its sector-specific focus;
- the collection, consolidation and codification of good practice;
- its use of general principles of sustainability;
- its underpinning by a series of case studies of good practice;
- its design as a management tool and based on a management systems approach;
- its emphasis on environmental assessment and improvement;
- its inclusion of performance target setting and monitoring.

The EMS has been developed in partnership with DGXI of the EU under the fifth environmental action plan and in consultation with stakeholders in the countryside, environmental and tourism sectors in the UK, Finland and Portugal.

The countryside EMS, in emphasizing the responsibility of management at the micro level of the site or organization, interprets the concept of sustainability widely. It recognizes that different priorities will exist in different areas, but suggests that systems should take account of the following aspects of sustainability:

1. The visitor impact on the immediate tourism site.
2. The off-site impacts of running the site.
3. The contribution to improvement of non-tourism environmental goals (e.g. sustainable forest management).
4. The contribution of site activities to the sustainability of the local economy.

The key aim of the countryside EMS is to ensure that its principles are incorporated into the corporate management system of the target organization. This should be reflected in the organisation's:

- mission;
- strategy;
- planning;
- operational targets;
- organizational structure;
- key tasks identified for personnel;
- review.

Among the benefits that such an approach can bring – over and above environmental improvements – are additional information to consumers, assistance in marketing, and help in the reduction of costs.

This book is divided into four parts. Part 1, 'Countryside, Leisure and the Environment' starts at the general level and then focuses on the local level. It is a synthesis of two strands. Chapter 1, 'Tourism and Recreation in the Countryside', investigates the range of tourism and recreation activities that are taking place in the countryside, with a particular emphasis on sites and destinations. Chapter 2 analyses environmental issues facing leisure and tourism at a general level. The strands of these two chapters are brought together in Chapter 3 where environmental management of tourism and recreation is analysed at a local level. This chapter, which is full of practical advice and case studies, concludes Part 1.

Part 2, 'Environmental Management Systems', sets out the justification for the rest of the book. There is no shortage of books about issues for environmental improvements for tourism and recreation in the countryside: what is missing is advice on how issues can be systemized and operationalized. Part 2, in analysing the Environmental Management Systems approach, provides an important framework and system by which environmental thinking and awareness achieved at a global, national and local level can be incorporated into the management of countryside destinations for tourism and recreation. In Chapter 4 the development and structure of Environmental Management Systems are discussed, whilst in Chapter 5 the effectiveness of an EMS is evaluated in relation to the range of other possible approaches.

Part 3, 'An EMS for Countryside Tourism and Recreation', contains five chapters that detail how an EMS can be put into place for countryside sites and destinations. It concentrates both on the development of an effective environmental management system and on how such a system can be utilized to achieve environmental improvement targets. It should be used in conjunction with Chapter 3.

Finally, Part 4 contains references and further reading, a glossary of terms, and addresses for contacts.

PART 1

COUNTRYSIDE, LEISURE AND THE ENVIRONMENT

Chapter 1

Tourism and Recreation in the Countryside

Objectives

The purpose of this chapter is to:

- outline the nature of tourism and recreation in the countryside;
- explain the importance of tourism and recreation for the countryside;
- define key concepts relating to this book;
- focus on management units as the targets for environmental management;
- analyse the activities and characteristics of tourism and recreation sites;
- provide case studies of businesses catering for visitors.

Introduction

The growing interest of nature and heritage has led to the buoyancy of special-interest tourism and activity holidays, turning the countryside into a key part in the recreation and tourism scene. The market for countryside tourism is growing across European countries. In the early 1990s a quarter of main holidays in Europe were spent in the countryside (Davidson, 1998), and the trend has been for the countryside to increase as a percentage of first holidays, and to consolidate itself as a major segment of second holidays and short breaks.

The increasing demand has meant that rural communities are using tourism and recreation as an economic development tool. The nature of the industry is one of small players using natural resources as their selling point; but the fact that natural resources are often available free of charge and visitors are hard to control means that the environment can pay a high price for short-term economic benefits. This chapter will investigate tourism and recreation and what they mean to the countryside. It will identify management units that actively cater for visitors by providing attractions, activities and services, and will argue that these sites have a responsibility for the environmental impacts caused by visitors. These sites will be the target for using Environmental Management Systems, and hence the focus of this book.

Defining tourism and recreation in the countryside

It is easier to discuss the positive and negative aspects of recreation and tourism in the countryside than to define any of the concepts involved. The countryside means many different things to many different people. The broadest definition is that it is rural, and therefore not urban (Williams, 1975; Sharpley and Sharpley, 1997) which, although being practical, leaves several questions unanswered. The countryside can also be defined as having characteristics in itself which are quite often related to the past. In that sense, it is referred to as a place that is unchanged, natural, but also as a place viewed as having certain society values, national identity and heritage. Increasingly it is seen as a refuge from modern, urban pressures, and this is reflected in the wish of many to exchange, albeit for limited periods of time, the man-made world and its associated demands of work and home, for the countryside. From that point of view, it is also seen as a nostalgic ideal of a better physical and social world (Bramwell, 1994).

In English, the word 'countryside' is mostly used to refer to the physical environment, whereas the word 'rural' focuses on the socio-economic environment (Gilg, 1996), but this difference does not exist in most European languages. This book will refer to countryside as those areas with low population density, small settlements, economies based on land production and traditional society structures (Lane, 1994), and refer to rural as activities and lifestyles in the countryside.

Similar difficulties occur when trying to define recreation and tourism and to consider their differences (McKercher, 1996). The traditional distinction is that recreation includes all activities carried out by day visitors, whereas to qualify to be a tourist you have to stay overnight. From the point of view of most suppliers of services in the countryside, the difference will not be so clear. Both tourism and recreation are central to the purposes of this book and it will only differentiate between day and overnight visitors if their behaviour or needs are different. Beyond definitions, what matters for the purposes of this book, is the impact that tourism and recreation are causing in the countryside.

The impact of tourism and recreation on the countryside

Rural Europe is going through a process of irreversible change. The loss of economic value of agricultural and forest land, together with the lack of interest in agriculture of younger generations has forced residents and governments alike to look for alternative sources of sustainable development. Tourism is increasingly used as one of the key development tools within rural Europe (WTO, 1996; Gannon, 1994; Lane, 1994; Williams and Shaw, 1988).

Tourism can provide supplementary income to existing rural businesses. During a period when traditional sources of revenue are under pressure, landowners are looking for alternative methods to generate extra revenue, and tourism is one of them. One of the achievements of tourism in the countryside is that, if planned appropriately, it can support inner rejuvenation of communities by bringing direct economic benefits to local farms and shops. Research on agricultural diversification suggests that around 15 per cent of farms in Britain provide some sort of tourism enterprise. The less accessible countryside relies even more strongly on tourism, as in the case of Cornwall in south-west England, where the figure rises to 35 per cent of farms (Denman, 1994). This is a common situation throughout Europe: three-quarters of Swiss small farms (under 15 hectares) could not survive without some sort of supplementary income, and as many as three-quarters of hill farmers can supplement their income through rural tourism (Leu, 1996). Countryside visitors are likely to be better off than average (CRN, 1996) and sports holidays in the outdoors usually yield higher expenditure (Mintel, 1996). Usually these are sports that are not expensive to cater for when visitors share facilities with the residents. This is exemplified by two Finnish farms in Case Study 1.1.

CASE STUDY 1.1

Diversification in Finnish farms into tourism and recreation

Log cabins were designed in keeping with the surroundings and built in the traditional Finnish style

Kantelesarkka farm is a family-owned business in East Finland that has traditionally relied on timber production (80 hectares), agriculture (16 hectares) and livestock. One partner works full time in the farm, while the second combines it with a part-time job in a neighbouring town. The farm sought and gained permission to diversify into trout fishing since second-home owners were interested in paying a reasonable sum to fish in their pools. This has now turned into the main source of income, catering for ice fishing in winter and pool fishing in summer. The couple has plans to combine the attraction of trout fishing with horse riding, either alone or in groups with a guide, and also hunting, picking berries and mushrooms. They consider that the key to turning the farm into a tourism business would be to develop self-catering accommodation.

Which is what the owners of the nearby farm Kokkolan Erä Ja Matkailu did. This 500 hectare farm was founded in the eighteenth century, and has historical buildings such as a windmill, a frame saw and a workshop, the oldest dating from 1811. Although most of the land is forested, the main income comes from tourism. The good location of the farm generated demand for overnight stays and outdoor recreation, and the owners built three log cabins in consecutive years. The cottages were to be built in a traditional style by the farm owner, yet to the highest comfort standards. The owners set aside 2 hectares of mature pines to be used for the main

structure of the cottages, and these were built using whole tree-trunks. It took a year to build each cottage: site selection, permissions and laying electricity cables took place in early autumn, road and ground preparation in late autumn, logwork in spring, and finishing the cottage in summer. The availability of accommodation has meant that the farm can provide other services. A smoke sauna was built, and this has proved very popular. The farm also caters for activities such as hunting, hiking and fishing, and in winter cross-country skiing and snowshoe walking.

Sources: Kantelesarkka, Kantelesärkän kalalaitos, 81220 Jakokoski, North Karelia, Finland, and Kokkolan Erä Ja Matkailu, Koivulahdentie 280, 81200 Eno, North Karelia, Finland

---

Bringing supplementary income to existing businesses is a key to stop emigration from rural areas in the long term. Yet some regions need to reverse the migration trends and attract new populations, and here the creation of new businesses, and associated employment opportunities, can help in the short to medium term. Rural tourism planners stress that local residents are usually less aware of new business opportunities, and that a large amount of new tourism business is developed by outsiders, and rural communities require training and support (Eden, 1996). Whether it is by residents in countryside areas diversifying into tourism, or newcomers starting new businesses, tourism is bringing life back into rural communities.

Despite the tempting beneficial economic impacts of tourism, countryside destinations need to take into account potential negative environmental and social externalities. Tourism can generate environmental impacts at a first stage of developing facilities and infrastructures, and at a second stage of usage of those facilities. Usage of facilities can cause several types of environmental impact: pollution caused by cars driving to the site, damage to the site's ecological environment, depletion of products and resources, and waste disposal. The exploitation of tourism and recreation can cause conflicts to arise with local communities who do not wish to see their countryside change. Global and site-specific environmental impacts will be reviewed in Chapters 2 and 3.

Visitors require transport and access routes to reach both attractions and services, and the majority of countryside holidays and days out are taken by independent tourists who drive from home to their accommodation centre, and only organized packages tend to rely on group transport. In Great Britain, about 50 per cent of day visits to woodlands and forests are by car, and this is usually when visits are further than 5 miles from home. Another 50 per cent of visits are on foot, but a large proportion of these are dog-walkers going less than 5 miles from their home (CRN, 1996).

Although tourism and recreation have the potential to generate fewer impacts than other forms of economic development, impacts still need managing. Sustainable approaches to tourism development encourage multiple use of resources that do not compromise the ability to meet four purposes: environmental conservation, economic production, achievement of social goals, and visitor enjoyment. This book will concentrate on environmental conservation through management, and the other three purposes will be considered only when there are overlaps.

Tourism and recreation sites as environmental management units

From the demand side, tourists say that they are going on holiday to the Alps, Lapland, the Black Forest, Snowdonia or Umbria, meaning a geographical area that is understood as an interesting place to go and that can fulfil their needs during their holiday. These needs will be access to the destination's attractions and activities, and services to cater for them during their stay. From the supply side, the destination is made up of a variety of usually small suppliers of those attractions, activities and services. Most suppliers are based in villages and rural towns, in the form of hotels, restaurants, cafes, museums and so on, since towns can absorb visitor requirements with fewer environmental impacts than new developments in the outdoors. The main emphasis in this book is placed in those tourism and recreation sites in outdoor settings, since the risk of impacts to the environment is greater. Outdoor recreational sites will be identifiable areas of land with a defined management unit, which can either be the owner or a contracting company. Since these sites are actively catering for visitors, they are implicitly accepting that they are responsible to manage the impacts caused by those visitors.

These sites will very often be the result of land set aside by the public sector or non-profit organizations for conservation and public enjoyment. Public sector provision of land, in the form of designated areas such as National Parks, concentrates tourists usually in sensitive places, and for this reason quiet enjoyment is promoted. At present there are around 200 National Parks in Europe, and hundreds other designated areas like natural reserves and parks, most of which have become tourist honeypots (FNNPE, 1993). Since conservation costs are high, the public sector is increasingly under pressure to partly self-finance the provision of recreational facilities, and therefore a large part of the services provided are leased out and the profits made from the lease are brought back to subsidize the cost of conservation.

Access to the countryside is seen as a public right, and tourists are not willing to pay purely for access (Beard, 1995). Since landowners are not making profit from simply allowing visitors to use their land, few encourage it. In order to compete with publicly owned sites providing free access, landowners have to provide activities and services that make the price paid worthwhile to the visitor. Putting these activities and services together under one site will usually take the shape of a tourist attraction or an accommodation centre. Case Study 1.2. shows a combination of a private–public partnership when setting up a new visitor centre to enjoy the countryside near Windsor, south-east England.

Academics debate about the appropriateness of some tourism and recreation developments in the countryside, and whether they can be classified as part of

CASE STUDY 1.2

Opening a forest to recreation near Windsor

Entrance to the Swinley Forest Discovery Outpost

The Windsor Great Park is the only Royal Park managed by The Crown Estate (UK) and consists of over 6,000 hectares, divided into forestry, gardens, parks and farming departments. 3,200 hectares of farming land are leased out, and at present commercial timber production is one of the main economic outputs. Since 1991 Swinley Forest (1,500 hectares) is a forest within the Great Park that combines timber production with recreation and includes a visitor centre. Situated in a densely populated residential area on the outskirts of London, with high demand for recreational land, the local government body was involved from the beginning. The car park,

educational and tourist facilities are owned by Bracknell Forest Borough Council, despite being in private land.

Initially all recreational activities were informal; but the unexpectedly high levels of use not only meant that greater management and control was needed to protect the environment and visitors, but also provided the opportunity to formalize recreation activities, such as mountain biking, horse riding, business management training and husky racing. A franchised hire shop supplies school groups and gives guided tours. The Crown Estate governors decided not to develop accommodation on site. At present there are more than

750,000 day visits per year, accounting for 5 per cent of the forests' income. All recreational activities are charged for except walking and car parking. With an average of 1,200 cars a day, parking revenue could generate £60,000 per year.

Usage pressures have forced management to zone users and activities. A number of space and time zones have been developed to define safe areas for certain activities and to reduce conflicts between different visitors, commercial timber production and conservation requirements. The needs of specific activities can be better provided for and more robust areas can be the focus for hard-wearing activities. It is easier and cheaper to monitor environmental damage and to develop actions to reduce these if they are focused in specific areas.

Some activities have been allocated specific zones, and nature trails and heritage trails have been defined. Cycling, in particular mountain biking, is the largest activity next to walking, and for that reason mountain bikers have specific routes planned for different competence levels. All bike users must have a permit to use the forest, that regulates users and also provides insurance to the cyclist against injury caused to a third person (under-12s do not require one). These are available daily (£1) or annually, through clubs affiliated with the site (for which a single £100 fee is paid to Windsor). In the same style horse riding is allowed through a permit scheme (normally annual), and husky racing has a specific zone and can only operate during specific times of the day.

Source: Crown Estate Office, The Great Park, Windsor, Berkshire, SL4 2HT

'rural tourism' just for being physically situated in a rural setting (e.g. Clark *et al.*, 1994; Lane, 1994). Countryside tourism and recreation can be understood in three different ways. First, all tourism and recreation activities taking place in a countryside setting. Second, a number of activities usually accepted by participants and providers as being 'rural'. Third, any activity taking place in any setting that participants perceive as rural and behave accordingly.

This book takes the broad perspective of including all activities sold in a countryside destination, whether these are using the countryside as a setting or whether the reason to visit is the natural and cultural heritage. The reason for including all of them is simply because they all need to be managed. If some tourism or recreation development is not appropriate to the rural setting, this should be picked up through the planning permission and pre-development environmental audit procedures, nowadays quite well established throughout Europe. If the argument as to what can be labelled as 'rural tourism' is a conceptual one, it is rather futile because the concept cannot be easily translated across European countries and languages, since each region understands rural tourism differently according to their background and resources. For example, in Switzerland rural tourism is interpreted as farm tourism (Leu, 1996:50) due to the importance of this type of activity, while in other areas it will be called green tourism, agritourism and so on, concepts with more specific meanings in English. Instead, this chapter will review two main components of tourism and recreation sites: first, the attractions and activities that draw people to the site; second, the services provided to enjoy those attractions.

The components of sites: activities, attractions and services

The majority of countryside sites are natural or cultural attractions in their own right, activity and sports centres, or accommodation centres that provide some outdoor entertainment. The list of potential activities is almost endless, but activities catered for at sites in Portugal, Great Britain and Finland include the following:

- abseiling;
- angling;
- archaeology;
- archery;
- ballooning;
- canoeing;
- caving and potholing;
- climbing;
- children's play areas;
- driving off-road vehicles;
- dog walking;
- field studies;
- flying microlights;
- flying model aeroplanes;
- golf;
- hang-gliding and paragliding;
- horse riding;
- hunting;
- husky sledding;
- jet skiing;
- motor sports;
- mountain biking;
- mushroom picking;
- orienteering;
- ornithology;
- paintball/war games;
- photography;
- picnicking;
- power boating;
- rafting;
- rowing;
- sailing and boardsailing;
- skiing;
- swimming;
- walking;
- running.

Despite such a long list of activities, the majority of holidays to the countryside are motivated by the passive enjoyment of nature and culture. In the United Kingdom, 20 per cent of all holidays (countryside and non-countryside) are activity focused, the most popular being walking holidays (see Table 1.1). Yet despite the fact that 80 per cent of tourists do not go on holiday to do a specific activity, at least over half the tourists participate in some outdoor activity while away (Mintel, 1998), which indicates the importance of participating in activities and sports during holidays. Hiking is by far the most popular outdoor activity in rural areas in countries as different as the UK and Norway (Mintel, 1998; Haukeland, 1998).

Tourism has traditionally received a higher profile than recreation, partly because its economic impacts are more obvious. Yet recreational visits are much more important in numbers, and less seasonal. For example, there are more than 900 million day visits to the countryside in Great Britain (CRN, 1996). As in the case of countryside holidays, walking is a key element to enjoying nature, as shown in Table 1.2.

Table 1.1 Participation in activities during holidays in the UK

	Main purpose (%)	Any participation (%)
Walking, hiking, rambling	5	16
Sailing, boating, canoeing, water sports	2	5
Fishing, hunting or shooting	2	4
Cycling	1	4
Nature/field study, wildlife, birdwatching	1	3
Golf	1	2
Climbing, mountain sports (abseiling, caving)	1	2
Horse riding, pony trekking	<1	1
Other activities	6	18
Any activity	**20**	**55**
No particular activity	**80**	**45**

Source: Adapted from Mintel (1998)

Table 1.2 Main purpose of recreation in British woods and forests (%)

Main purpose	Woods/forests
Walk/ramble/hill walk	57
Drive, picnic or sightseeing	7
Hobby/special interest	6
Countryside sport (not at particular facility, e.g. fishing, sailing, horse riding . . .)	5
Visit friends' and relatives' home	5
Eat out or drink	4
Cycling/mountain biking	4
Outdoor sport (sports centre, ground, stadium or club)	4
Visit tourist/recreational attraction	3
Informal sport/children's games	2
Watch sport	1
Other	2

Source: CRN (1996)

A large number of the recreational activities that take place in settings such as woodlands, for example picnicking, could also take place elsewhere; but they are enhanced by the natural surroundings (Font and Tribe, 2000). This could be said about the countryside in general, which is often used as a pleasant backstage for recreational activities. Illustrations here show an interpretive tableau in a forest outside Bologna (Italy) showing the carbon-making process and the centrepiece of the Mabinogion sculpture trail at the Cwmcarn Forest Drive (South Wales), representing one of the characters from the Celtic folklore tales, and used as an educational tool for children.

Although most countryside recreation activities listed are outdoors, indoor activities could arguably be included. For example, there is a great growth for farm attractions mostly for the family market, where farm life and farming practices are

Attractions can be developed around educational activities and interpretation

interpreted in a more or less formal manner for the entertainment and education of visitors (Denman, 1994). Interpreting rural heritage through traditional settlements in the countryside can include many more aspects than just farm life and diversify into explaining about rural life, mining, fishing, wine, olive oil, timber, railways, crafts and traditions, to mention a few. The list of countryside attractions gets even longer if these are included, and the setting and design of the attraction will have a great influence in whether the attraction is perceived as rural. In most cases the same site will provide a combination of formal and informal activities and attractions, as seen in Case Study 1.3

Sites need services to allow people to participate in activities or enjoy the attractions. The range of services that visitors may need is quite varied, and includes accommodation, food retail outlets, parking, equipment hire, souvenir and convenience shops, footpaths and toilets, to name a few. Denman (1994) suggests that eating farm food and locally produced meals is one of the key ingredients to the rural experience sought by visitors, and it could be argued that these could be almost a tourist attraction in itself. France is one of the countries already ahead in the standardization of this idea though the concept of Ferme Auberges (farm restaurants). Indeed a large part of the 'rural souvenirs' relate to locally produced food.

CASE STUDY 1.3

Providing family-run recreational facilities in the woodland

Wilderness Wood is a family-run working woodland of chestnut coppice and pine and beech plantations situated in the Weald of Sussex, south-east England. Woodlands in this area used to produce charcoal to fuel the iron, glass, hop-drying, gunpowder and brickwork industries. Today the majority of these woods stand unmanaged as historic relics. Coppicing, the traditional technique to manage the local woodlands, is too labour intensive to make timber production economically feasible when both alternative materials and imported timber are cheaper.

The owners see their woodland as a uniquely adaptable multi-purpose resource that can produce sustainable raw materials (wood and timber) as well as providing for recreation and enjoyment, and conserving wildlife and landscape. Coppicing techniques have been reinstated, making use of the tendency of broad-leaved trees to re-sprout from the stump. These produce poles that can be easily cut and moved by hand. This small timber is used to produce garden furniture, trellis panels, rose arches, fence poles and many garden accessories. These products are designed and manufactured on site to order and then stocked and sold on site.

School visits take place during the week, and children are encouraged to learn about these traditional techniques. Family visits concentrate on weekends, when staff concentrate on preparing activities, preparing light meals and selling some of the products produced from timber. Demand is entirely fuelled by their recreational visitors and currently outstrips supply, showing that there still is a way to make a profit from traditional coppiced woodland. The proximity to London and to the south coast of England ensure there is demand all year round, although the busiest periods are spring, summer and a short spell before Christmas for families coming to dig up their own Christmas tree.

Source: Wilderness Wood, Uckfield, Sussex, TN22 4HJ

Not all facilities will be available in every site, and in general availability will depend on the length of stay and the type of activity. A National Park may cater for day visitors by having toilets, a visitor centre, walking trails and picnic tables, whereas a forest holiday centre will cater for overnight visitors by providing accommodation and a variety of entertainment and activities. The majority of tourism and recreation providers cater primarily for a car-driving market, which poses pressures on parking provision and also causes environmental impacts.

A large percentage of visitors will not travel unless there is a minimum amount of infrastructures, such as electricity, water, sewage and waste disposal, which require high investment and are potentially impacting. Yet sites should preserve the feeling of natural landscape, and therefore when facilities are required in the countryside, present structures such as bunkhouses, barns and farms that would otherwise be run down should be used. One of the most important contributions that farms can provide to tourism development is the provision of

Traditional food is one of the key attractions to rural tourism

Trywyn Forest (Mid-Wales) renovated these once run-down barns into holiday homes to diversify from their timber-producing main business

accommodation, which in countries like Austria is as high as 18 per cent of the country's bedspaces (Embacher, 1994). A good example can be seen in Case Study 1.4, where hunting tourism has been used to regenerate run-down farm sites in Portugal. If new development is the only choice, it should be in keeping with local traditional styles, rather than upstaging the landscape (Bell, 1997; Gunn, 1994).

Summary

Tourism and recreation in the countryside encompass a large number of activities taking place in a setting that is hard to define. The myriad of players and providers

CASE STUDY 1.4

Hunting tourism in South Portugal

The Monte de Marvila is part of a recreation network in Alentejo (South Portugal) which offers organized and diverse recreational activities. Marvila, a rural area consisting of forests and agricultural land, results from the union of four non-fenced properties, owned by several families, in a total area of 3,000 hectares. Marvila was always a place where forestry, pasture, hunting and horse breeding were the traditional activities. European funds have helped the owners to re-establish traditional activities, firstly through reafforesting the area and, after 1995, developing small-scale tourism accommodation and activities. Many other similar farms can be found in South Portugal.

The traditional activities are the great attraction of this place. Hunting is highly valued and includes partridge, hare, wild rabbit, pigeon, dove and fox hunting. Lusi-tanian horse breeding also attracts many people, good facilities have made horse trials and other equestrian activities very popular. In recent years more activities and amenities have been put in place for visitors to walk, take photos, mountain bike, go on balloon trips, follow nature trails or join guided historical and cultural heritage tours. The proximity to Montargil's dam is an opportunity to practise several water-sports such as sailing and jet skiing. A guide is provided for most activities; this guarantees a high quality service and is a way to monitor and control impacts caused from recreational pursuits. This project also has a positive impact on the local community, providing seasonal employment and custom for their services.

Source: Casa Vaz Monteiro, Campo Grande, n° 30, 3°G, 1700 Lisboa, Portugal

makes it difficult to put boundaries to this industry, let alone identify responsibilities relating to the environmental management of the resources used. Yet environmental pressures relating to the provision of tourism and recreation are increasing and the question cannot be postponed.

This book follows the approach that environment management of land resources used for tourism should be the responsibility of the management unit running those resources, and environmental management performance should be assessed at the tourist/recreation site level. This approach will at least work for those landowners promoting tourism and recreation, since they are implicitly accepting the impacts caused by visitors. This chapter provides a baseline description of the type of sites the rest of the book will refer to and will target. The nature, ownership and components of these sites are reviewed, with special emphasis on the attractions, activities and services that sites may provide for visitors.

Chapter 2

Environmental Issues for Tourism and Recreation

Objectives

The objectives of this chapter are to:

- analyse the relationship between tourism and recreation and major environmental issues;
- analyse tourism and recreation in the context of the general issue of sustainable development;
- examine the international community's responses to environmental issues;
- consider implications for policy development and implementation;
- examine the environmental pressures and challenges facing leisure and recreation from a corporate perspective.

Introduction

In recent decades increasing attention has been paid to the effects of human activities on the environment. Concerns are growing over the possible consequences for our global life-support systems if patterns of environmentally disruptive and destructive economic development similar to those witnessed thus far should continue into the future. Opinions vary as to the seriousness of environmental problems, but at the very least such issues raise important questions about the quality of life that can be expected by current and future inhabitants of this planet.

The realization of the need to guard against environmental degradation has led to certain forms of economic activity coming under increasing scrutiny. Pressures are growing on industries for the environment to be given a higher priority when policies are being developed and performance is being measured.

Companies in high-profile industries whose actual or potential environmental impacts are severe, such as oil companies and chemical manufacturers, often face strict laws and stringent controls which govern their activities, with harsh penalties and adverse publicity should they fail to operate to required standards. Many have responded to the challenges they face by making significant and demonstrable progress where their environmental performance is concerned, and have pledged commitment towards further, far-reaching improvements. The tourism and recreation sector, however, has largely escaped the close attention paid to many other industry sectors where environmental performance is concerned.

The environmental effects created by the tourism and recreation sector seem on the whole rather indistinct, insignificant and diffuse, contrasting starkly with the more obvious effects produced by many other industries. When compared with the oil and chemical industries, for example, those environmental threats and problems posed by the likes of hotel chains, golf courses, theme parks and holidays in the sun are not so readily apparent; or, even if they are recognized, they do not seem as menacing. The realization has dawned, however, that such a large and growing sector does indeed have cumulative influences on the environment which, by virtue of the sector's sheer size and scale, are not confined to local and regional effects but are indeed truly global in their significance.

Relationships between tourism and recreation and key environmental issues

Surveys of public attitudes to the environment reflect the fact that environmental issues, whether local or global in nature, have become ingrained in the public consciousness. The UK Department of Transport, Environment and the Regions, in one of its more recent public attitude surveys, reported that significant numbers of people – 60 per cent or more of those surveyed – were 'very worried' about chemicals in rivers or the sea, sewage on beaches or in bathing waters, and dangerous waste. About 50 per cent were similarly concerned about traffic fumes and smog, ozone layer depletion and species loss. Approximately one-third of those surveyed were very worried about global warming and acid rain (DETR, 1998). Add on the percentages of those who were merely 'worried' about the above issues, rather than 'very worried', and the total levels of concern are revealed to be even higher.

The tourism and recreation industry contributes to some degree to all of the issues referred to above, and, of course, it may be adversely affected in various ways by such issues. These links are increasingly acknowledged by elements of the industry; the World Travel and Tourism Environment Research Centre (WTTERC), for example, have elucidated the relationships between travel and tourism and key environmental issues such as global warming, ozone layer depletion, acid rain, resource consumption and pollution of air and water (WTTERC, 1993).

As an increasingly significant component of economic activity world-wide, tourism and recreation certainly contributes to environmental problems, but what is the extent of this contribution? There are no easy ways of demonstrating in measurable or unequivocal terms the significance of those environmental effects created by such a huge and diverse sector. However, if it can be established with reasonable clarity that the tourism and recreation industry does indeed contribute significantly to environmental problems, then the onus clearly rests with those involved in the industry to recognize and meet their environmental obligations.

The climate change issue

One example of a clear relationship between tourism and recreation and environmental issues is that of the aviation industry and concerns over its contribution to climate change. British Airways figures for 1996, for example, indicated that about 65 per cent of their passengers were leisure travellers and that this percentage was growing (British Airways, 1996).

Air traffic generally has grown by around 9 per cent a year since 1960, and is set to continue to rise by about 3 per cent per year over the next 50 years (ENDS, 1999). Like any industry that burns fossil fuel, the aviation industry creates emissions of gases such as carbon dioxide (CO_2) that are believed to cause climate change. Based on figures for 1997–8, the mainline services of British Airways alone led to an estimated output of carbon dioxide into the atmosphere of over 16 million tonnes, in addition to high levels of other undesirable emissions such as nitrogen oxides (British Airways, 1998).

A 1999 report from the Intergovernmental Panel on Climate Change estimates the overall contribution of aircraft to be around 3.5 per cent of all human impact on climate change, an effect which is anticipated to increase four-fold over the next 50 years, even making allowances for design and efficiency improvements (ENDS, 1999). Clearly, much of the present and predicted impact on the stability of the global climate from this source alone may be attributed to tourism and recreation industry activity.

The environmental effects resulting from the activities of providers of tourism and recreation facilities and products are often not immediately apparent and may consequently be considered insignificant. The issue of energy consumption, particularly electricity use, is arguably one that seldom receives the attention that it should, considering its implications for the environment. Global electricity demand is rising, and this demand is being met chiefly (roughly 70 per cent) through the use of power stations that burn fossil fuels such as coal, natural gas and oil. The combustion of these leads to emissions of carbon dioxide (CO_2) and other gases that may contribute, among other problems, to climate change.

Much of this electricity demand is being created, directly or indirectly, by the tourism and recreation sector. When the energy demands of operators and providers in the tourism and recreation sector as a whole are taken into account, the implications for the global atmosphere are obviously highly significant.

The activities of operators and providers referred to above have, until quite recently, been regarded as routine and acceptable business behaviour; they were simply a large-scale reflection of what we as individuals do in society: consume energy and generate transport emissions. The environmental implications of such activities were either not generally recognized or were not given a high priority.

The links between issues such as climate change and our actions, whether as individuals or large corporations, are now increasingly understood, however. There is a growing expectation within society generally that activities that are clearly contributing to environmental problems should be addressed and modified accordingly.

The energy requirements of individual visitor amenities add up to a significant global total

Other environmental issues

The involvement of tourism and recreation with other environmental issues is wide ranging and many examples exist, such as those highlighted in case 2.1, of relationships that are direct and obvious, as well as many that are indirect and less readily apparent. The sector to some degree contributes to all of the major issues of global significance, as well as to many important regional and local issues, through activities such as transport, energy consumption and waste generation.

A lorry taking waste from a countryside recreation site

CASE STUDY 2.1

Recreational trampling and compaction

A popular spot at Burnham Beeches where trampling has resulted in erosion, soil compaction, root exposure and tree death

Problems

Damage to trees caused by trampling can range from arrested development to death.

Causes

Recreational trampling can have an effect on many types of woodland soil and vegetation. The degree of impact is related to intensity and regularity of use, the numbers involved in any given area and environmental factors, particularly slope, wetness of the ground and soil type. Impact is also related to the nature of the woodland species, since some are more vulnerable than others. Those woodland species which are adapted to the low levels of light beneath the woodland canopy, are most vulnerable to damage.

Compaction is the most noted effect on forest soils resulting from recreational trampling. The pore space in soils is directly affected by compaction. Initially the large macropores are reduced, which results in air and water movement being restricted to micropores. As compaction increases, aeration decreases and becomes the most limiting factor in root elongation. At high compaction levels, roots are restricted to cracks and can barely penetrate the soil matrix. Possible impacts include a decrease in root branching and the number of feeder rootlets. Where root exposure results from trampling, compaction is compounded by abrasion. Forest areas most likely to be affected are trails, picnic areas, campsites, and star attractions.

Solutions

Approaches to this problem include tree management and visitor management. Visitor management can involve the diverting of paths, relocation of activities, and fencing around trees under threat.

At Sherwood Forest trampling damage threatens a line of ancient oaks. These oaks have already undergone extensive tree surgery and it is now planned to divert a heavily used footpath to ease compaction damage. The Major Oak is Sherwood Forest's star attraction and can attract up to 1 million visitors a year: popularity stems from legend that Robin Hood hid from his enemies inside this tree. Trampling and compaction mean that the immediate vicin- ity of the tree has now been fenced off. To encourage recovery the area has been mulched. The use of explanatory signage to explain the fencing policy plays an impor- tant role in encouraging the co-operation of visitors.

Sherwood Forest's Major Oak is supported and fenced to extend its life. As a result it must be viewed from a distance

Tree surgery has been needed to save Sherwood Forest's ancient oaks from soil compaction caused by the use of the nearby trail. It is now planned to divert the path

Signage reinforces the message of the physical boundary around The Druids Oak at Burnham Beeches

Tourism, recreation and sustainable development

As indicated in the previous section, the links between tourism and recreation and specific environmental issues can be readily demonstrated. In some cases, tourism and recreation contributes to environmental problems in much the same way as does society in general, while in other cases certain problems can be attributed much more specifically to this sector.

However, it is now commonly recognized that specific environmental problems may be just the individual symptoms of a broader underlying condition: a pattern of economic development that is in the long term environmentally, socially and even economically unsustainable. The general trend followed by economic development globally has been the large-scale consumption of environmental resources. By developing in a manner that relies on sizeable inputs from the environment in terms of land, minerals, fuels, water and other resources, equally sizeable outputs and consequences have also been generated in terms of land degradation, habitat and species loss, atmospheric pollution, contamination of water resources, waste production and so on.

Economic and other human activities do not function in a vacuum: they ultimately depend on and are supported by resources provided by the environment, and nowhere is this more evidently the case than where tourism and recreation is concerned.

Environmental resources are consumed to provide the inputs to the development process, but the overall burden on the environment is increased still further because resources are also consumed by the outputs of the process. For example, areas of land and sea-bed are 'consumed' to make way for oil extraction, and the oil itself for the most part is ultimately consumed in combustion engines for transport purposes. When oil is burned, the atmosphere is consumed in that it is used as a dumping ground for waste emissions and is consequently degraded as a resource that can supply other functions, such as providing safe, breathable air.

Clearly, if essential environmental resources cannot be adequately sustained, they in turn cannot sustain economic and other human activity. The imperative has emerged, therefore, to adopt patterns of development that can fulfil socio-economic objectives without reducing the ability of natural resources to sustain us in the long term: this goal is referred to as sustainable development.

There are many socio-economic and environmental issues associated with sustainable development, but a key area of concern is the use of renewable resources as opposed to ones that can be depleted and are non-renewable: oil and coal are obvious examples of the latter type.

Some resources are inherently renewable, there being little that mankind could do to deplete or degrade them: wind and solar energy are examples. Other resources, though, are renewable but capable of being depleted if they are over-exploited and badly managed: air, water and soil are examples, together with biological resources such as forests and other habitats, fish stocks and species in general. These renewable but depletable resources can, in theory, be consumed indefinitely provided they are managed carefully. Selman (1992) provides a useful summary classification of the different resources.

Using renewable energy: pedal power

Sustainability indicators

One of the widely accepted indicators of whether society is operating on a more sustainable footing is the extent to which renewable resources are being used as balanced against non-renewable resource consumption. Another indicator of sustainability would be the status of those depletable but theoretically renewable resources. Unfortunately, losses of topsoil from agricultural systems, losses of water resources, virgin forests and species diversity are just a few examples that bear testament to the need for improved management of renewable natural resources. Ideally, stocks of renewable resources should be stable or increasing.

Transport

The 1998 'Transport Trends' report from the UK government, the latest in a series of such reports, indicated that in 1996 the average number of car journeys per person for leisure purposes was well in excess of 300. This figure is significantly higher than any of the other reasons given for car travel, such as school runs, business and shopping (Worpole, 1999). Transport statistics for 1995–6 show that the average British resident travelled nearly 6,700 miles per year, with car and van usage accounting for 82 per cent of total mileage travelled. Car usage in general is increasing (DETR, 1998).

It is clearly the case that the level of use of road transport for tourism and recreation purposes, whilst difficult to quantify in precise terms, forms a very significant proportion of overall vehicle usage and is therefore responsible for a similar proportion of vehicle-related pollution and other impacts.

The proportion of energy consumed by transport in the UK is steadily rising. By 1997, transport was consuming more than one-third of all energy used in the UK, representing the burning of some 53 million tonnes of oil equivalent (DETR, 1998). The consumption of a finite resource to this extent, with its attendant environmental consequences, is clearly an activity that conflicts with the basic principles of sustainable development.

It could be reasonably argued that those operators involved in areas of the industry that encourage the use of road transport, particularly private car use, should not ignore this issue simply because it may be difficult to precisely identify and quantify tourism and recreation's contribution to road transport impacts.

It was indicated earlier that companies in the aviation industry, such as British Airways, function largely due to leisure demands. Figures for 1997–8 reveal that British Airways mainline services consumed 5.3 million tonnes of fuel, an increase of 6.1 per cent on the previous year. The figures for 1996–7 likewise show a similar increase compared to the previous year (British Airways, 1998; British Airways, 1997).

The aviation industry is reliant on kerosene-based (oil-derived) fuel to run its aircraft. Where road transport is concerned, considerable research is under way to develop alternative propulsion systems that are based to varying degrees on renewable resources. Some vehicles already exist, albeit mainly at prototype stages, that do not require fossil fuels in order to run. On the other hand, the aviation industry appears to have no alternative to kerosene-based fuel in sight, and thus seems set to remain fundamentally unsustainable for the foreseeable future.

Many visitors to the countryside arrive by car

Use of public transport and coach travel can reduce car use in the countryside

Energy supply and demand

The energy supply for tourism and recreation companies comes from a variety of sources, but at present the vast majority of this energy is supplied from non-renewable sources. Until operators requiring high energy input, such as theme parks, holiday villages and hotels, are supplied using resources that are renewable, and therefore potentially sustainable, this will remain a major area of leisure-related activity which is far from being in harmony with the ideals of sustainable development.

The brief examples above are intended to show that many leisure-related activities that have long been regarded as normal and acceptable actually do give rise to a variety of environmental and other impacts, and in addition are often inherently unsustainable.

There is a growing awareness that many of our actions, however mundane and commonplace, have environmental implications that cannot be ignored. Priorities are changing, and if we accept the need as individuals to behave more responsibly in order to sustain environmental resources and protect environmental quality, then it is certainly expected that organizations, whether public or private, large or small, should also demonstrate more responsible attitudes and behaviour. Some key responses made by organizations at all levels to environmental challenges are examined in the following sections.

Environmental policy development and implementation

The development of policies to address environmental problems is now commonplace among organizations of all kinds. Policy development does not take place in isolation however; there are always external considerations for organizations to take into account, not least of which is the need to address and harmonize with the overarching policy aims created by the international community. International environmental policy increasingly informs and directs policy formulation at national and local government levels and within the private sector.

Concerns relating to environmental problems induced by mankind have existed for almost as long as there have been human societies and settlements. Plato was alarmed over the soil erosion resulting from woodland clearance to make way for agriculture on the hillsides around Athens. There were complaints in fifth-century Rome about the pollution of the river Tiber. Problems with air quality resulting from open coal furnaces led to their prohibition by Edward I in 1306 in London, one of the earliest examples of statutory anti-pollution measures (Kiss and Shelton, 1997).

While the examples above reflect human concern about certain localized environmental problems, many other significant and more widespread impacts on the environment were occurring. These were not at the time regarded as issues because they were not perceived as threatening enough by individual communities or societies to require any modification of human behaviour. Losses of resources such as species and habitats are prime examples of impacts which have historically received relatively little serious attention until recently.

There have been gradually increasing levels of concern that human activity is impacting upon the environment on a global scale. Whilst problems at local and even national levels have been relatively easy to control through state intervention of some kind, problems at a global level require international co-operation in order to be addressed adequately. This principle gained international recognition and acceptance at the United Nations Conference on the Human Environment held in Stockholm in 1972.

The Stockholm Conference

Principles relating to co-operation and improved international management regarding the global environment were agreed by many world leaders at Stockholm in 1972 (Birnie and Boyle, 1992). These agreements, however, appeared for some time to be rather limited in terms of improving environmental protection. Most environmental problems remained unchanged or even worsened in the years that followed, despite this ground-breaking conference. However, the Stockholm gathering had outcomes that led in the long term to significant developments. For example, the leaders of the European Community were considerably influenced by the Stockholm conference and subsequently began to formulate and implement the EC's own environmental policy.

Another important outcome of the Stockholm conference was the creation of the United Nations Environment Programme (UNEP). One of UNEP's key roles is to monitor, assess and report on the state of the global environment (Kiss and Shelton, 1997). In the years that followed, it was largely UNEP's reporting of the deterioration of many aspects of the global environment that convinced the international community of the need for further and more serious action to address environmental issues.

Growing concerns

The Apollo space missions in the late 1960s played a significant role in changing attitudes, allowing for the first time a view of Earth looking back from space. The image of a small, blue ball standing out against the cold, dark immensity of space did much to popularize the understanding of the Earth as a provider of life-support systems on which mankind is undeniably and inescapably reliant.

The pressures put on environmental resources by human demands appeared to be putting at risk the stability of these global life-support systems. Various forms of air pollution from an increasing number of sources, depletion and contamination of fresh water supplies and loss of topsoil from agricultural systems were among many such problems. The pressures on the global environment seemed likely to increase, considering a rapidly expanding world population and a pattern of development that generally demanded energy supply and consumption of materials and other resources on a large scale.

Many indicators of human welfare monitored by UNEP and other organizations seemed to confirm the potential for human influence to threaten the ability of the environment to support life. Comparing the 1970s with the previous decade, for example, considerably more people were at risk from disasters associated with environmental mismanagement such as droughts and floods (WCED, 1987). These trends have been maintained to the present day (Brown, 1999), and problems such as hunger and poverty, in terms of absolute numbers of people affected, are more prevalent today than ever before.

The Brundtland Commission

Adverse impacts on human welfare tend to hinder economic progress and social stability. Growing acceptance became evident among world leaders that attempts to achieve development would be ultimately unsuccessful if there was inadequate provision for environmental protection, which in turn would damage the prospects for improving human welfare.

The crucial nature of the links between environment and development were explicitly acknowledged by the United Nations in 1983 when the 'Brundtland Commission', the World Commission on Environment and Development (WCED), was established. The Commission's task was to formulate 'a global agenda for change' and recommend strategies for achieving development in a fashion that could be sustainable rather than ultimately self-defeating (WCED, 1987).

The WCED duly produced a report in 1987, 'Our Common Future', which carefully explains and advocates the need for sustainable development, defined as that which 'meets the needs of the present without compromising the ability of future generations to meet their own needs' (WCED, 1987).

'Our Common Future' was extremely influential as a publication in its own right, informing policy-making in organizations and governments at all levels. To properly address the issues involved in creating an institutional framework that could encourage and enable sustainable development to occur, the United Nations convened a Conference on Environment and Development – an Earth Summit – in Rio de Janeiro, 1992.

The Earth Summit

A catalogue of environmental accidents, disasters and problems, often at high human cost, had been highlighted in the decade leading up to the Earth Summit. In addition to specific incidents such as Bhopal (1984), Chernobyl (1986) and the Exxon Valdez oil spill (1989), there were other life-threatening, global-scale issues causing concern, such as ozone layer depletion and climate change.

The 1992 Earth Summit, like many international gatherings before and since, produced agreements to deal with specific issues; the Framework Convention on Climate Change and the Convention on Biological Diversity are examples of treaties that emerged from the Summit. Procedures were also established which would facilitate future international co-operation and agreement on environmental issues.

However, it might be argued that the most significant outcome of the Earth Summit was Agenda 21, a comprehensive action plan dealing with the broad range of issues involving development and environment. Agenda 21 sets out guidelines for the global community to work towards sustainable development up to the twenty-first century and beyond.

At Rio, 182 governments signalled their commitment to sustainable development by adopting Agenda 21. In line with these commitments, many countries have prepared national sustainable development strategies and action plans to implement them. The UK published its strategy for sustainable development in 1994. This strategy examines the arrangements and processes necessary for carrying forward sustainable development in the different sectors of society. One key sector identified is leisure, and the strategy exhorts those within the leisure industry to become more aware of the environmental consequences of their activities (DoE, 1994).

To measure progress, the UK government has since established indicators of sustainable development for the UK, where key objectives and issues are identified, together with the means by which performance relating to these is to be assessed (DETR, 1998).

Regional and local government bodies have also embraced the principles of sustainable development; virtually all local authorities in the UK, for example, have prepared their own local Agenda 21 programmes which are informing and directing policies at the local level.

In order to monitor and review progress made by countries on the implementation of Agenda 21, the Commission on Sustainable Development was created by the UN in the aftermath of the Earth Summit. This Commission also has a co-ordinating role within the UN framework, overseeing and monitoring the implementation of Agenda 21 by many of the key UN agencies and organizations, including the World Bank and UNEP.

The European dimension

The development and application of environmental policy in member states of the European Union (EU) is greatly affected by EU policy. New legislation and initiatives being enacted within member states mainly emanate from EU policy, so the direction and force of EU policy is a fundamental consideration when the environmental policy framework which operates within individual member states is examined.

By 1972, environmental concerns had grown sufficiently that EU policy on the environment was established. Economic expansion for its own sake was declared not to be in the interests of the EU and its people unless it occurred in harmony with improved quality of life and environmental protection (Kiss and Shelton, 1997). Thus the Community was already predisposed towards the principles that were later to be expounded in Agenda 21.

Far-reaching developments occurred with the 1986 Single European Act, where the EU explicitly committed itself to give high priority to environmental protection. Further, environmental considerations were to be integrated into the development and implementation of all other relevant EU policies.

In order to implement its policy principles, Action Programmes on the Environment were adopted by the EU, the first beginning in 1973. The Fifth Action Programme (5th AP), running from 1993–2000, went further than any of the previous programmes to integrate environmental considerations into all EU decision-making. This Programme is entitled 'Towards Sustainability', reflecting the fact that it is part of the EU's response to Agenda 21.

The 5th AP addresses five target sectors for special attention, largely 'because they were believed to be crucial in the attempt to change our current economic model into a more sustainable one' (Commission of the European Communities, 1997). The sectors chosen were manufacturing industry, energy, transport, agriculture, and tourism.

The latter was singled out partly because, according to World Tourism Organisation figures, tourism was likely to be the largest single economic activity in the EU by 2000, with an annual growth rate of tourist arrivals in Europe being steadily maintained at about 3.5 per cent (Commission of the European Communities, 1997). It should be remembered from the discussion earlier, however, that manufacturing industry, energy and transport are all sectors where tourism and recreation is, directly or indirectly, heavily involved. The 5th AP acknowledges that the real problems causing environmental loss and damage are current patterns of human consumption and behaviour. Another significant element of current and future EU policy is the broadening of the range of measures to be applied, involving the use of market-based incentives in addition to tough legal measures.

Governments at national, regional and local levels continue to pass laws and take actions in response to particular problems or issues that concern them. However, national and local environmental objectives are increasingly coming into line with those of the international community, especially where member states of the EU are concerned.

Policy principles

The recognition of environmental threats has led to certain guiding principles becoming established which help to inform and direct the policy-making process. These principles have found expression through many forms of action taken at international through to local level. Though often embodied in laws, these principles are increasingly applied where any form or level of decision-making in relation to environmental matters is concerned. The following are examples of key policy principles:

Conservation of environmental resources

Conservation as a policy is a long-established approach to environmental protection. In a general sense such a policy may be aiming to achieve the sustainable management of renewable resources such as soil, forests and fisheries. More specifically, conservation policies involve the designation of protected status for landscapes, habitats or individual species; as more of these resources are lost or threatened, the importance of conservation is increased.

The application of conservation policies to attempt to preserve or manage specific components of the environment, however, is an approach which is rather limited when dealing with more complex, general issues such as environmental quality or certain specific issues such as climate change.

Improvement of environmental quality

Sustainable development implies a continual improvement in quality of life. This is not realistically feasible unless many aspects of environmental quality are improved beyond current levels. Many polluted rivers have been made cleaner and air quality in some respects has been improved in many towns and cities;

these are examples where social, economic and environmental objectives clearly converge.

Resolving cases where, say, economic objectives appear to conflict with environmental protection has often proved difficult and proactive policies that are intended to create improved environmental quality may require significant realignment of social and economic objectives. It is worth noting that the EU is strongly committed to take positive action to improve the environment and quality of life, and many of its policies are adapted to accommodate these aims.

Preventing environmental damage

'Prevention is better than cure' is the first policy principle laid out in the EU's action programme aims in 1973 (Haigh, 1992). Curbing actions that might result in unnecessary or unwanted damage appears to be a matter of common sense, but short-term economic gain has often been given priority over possible harm done to the environment. Also, the consequences of actions are not always clear due to a lack of existing knowledge. For example, the widespread use of chlorofluorocarbons (CFCs) in various applications, such as their role as cooling agents in air-conditioning and refrigeration systems, led to deleterious effects on the ozone layer that were largely unpredicted by the scientific community for many years.

Where harmful environmental effects are identifiable, those actions responsible are often subject to 'command and control' legislation to prevent the creation of pollution and nuisances at source. As knowledge about environmental problems has grown, so has the range and strength of measures in line with this approach to environmental protection.

The precautionary principle

As indicated in the previous section, clear proof of the environmental consequences of actions may not be immediately evident. However, it is increasingly accepted that a lack of scientific certainty should not be used as a reason for postponing measures to prevent serious environmental harm (OECD, 1990). The application of this principle in policies at all levels leads to a presumption in favour of protecting the environment over the continuation of any activities that are seen as potentially threatening to environmental well-being.

The 'polluter pays' principle

The growing fields of environmental economics and accounting acknowledge the principle that pricing of goods and services should reflect the true social costs of their production and use (Pearce *et al.*, 1989). The Organisation for Economic Co-operation and Development has long been concerned that distortions in international trade might occur or unfair competitive advantage could be gained if countries allowed their industries to freely create pollution without bearing at least some of the costs (OECD, 1975). The European Community likewise included the principle in its action programme aims in 1973 (Haigh, 1992).

This policy approach is now finding expression through many laws and initiatives at national, regional and local level. In the UK, for example, increased costs of waste disposal as a result of the 1995 landfill tax and the forthcoming energy tax are just two of the growing number of manifestations of this policy. These examples indicate that companies in all sectors are affected by this policy approach – as indeed are individual consumers – as true environmental costs are increasingly reflected in the provision and use of goods and services. For producers and consumers alike, 'cost implications should be brought home directly to the people responsible' (DoE, 1994).

Incentive-based policies

These are considered in Chapter 5.

The policy–reality interface

Those involved in the tourism and recreation industry need to take into account the overarching policy context set by governments with which their own policies need to be harmonized. Organizations exist to help them do this, serving as policy interpreters and facilitators.

At the international level, a prominent example is the World Tourism Organisation (WTO), which is the established inter-governmental agency for travel and tourism policies worldwide. The WTO has links with UNEP, and, among many other activities, has developed indicators of sustainable development for the travel and tourism industry. In addition, UNEP itself has recently provided a report on ecolabelling practices in tourism, with a view to helping governments, industry operators and other organizations to use this approach to steer tourism closer to sustainability (UNEP, 1998).

At the national level are agencies that work on behalf of the government to promote the application of policy within their respective remits. In England, for example, the Countryside Commission, Rural Development Commission, English Tourist Board and Department of Culture, Media and Sport are just some of the government agencies whose activities are relevant to tourism and recreation to a greater or lesser degree.

In order to increase the validity and effectiveness of their actions and recommendations, horizontal integration is often undertaken between such agencies, where they co-operate in the production and dissemination of reports and best-practice guidelines for those involved in the tourism and recreation industry. The four agencies referred to above, for example, jointly produced 'Sustainable Rural Tourism: Opportunities for local action', a report which examines the relevant government policies and translates the principles concerned into practical applications in the rural context (Countryside Commission, 1995). Local authorities also are often heavily involved in creating local responses to national and international policies; local Agenda 21 programmes particularly have resulted in a proliferation of initiatives.

Representative trade bodies are also active in terms of providing support and

advice for their members where environmental policy development and application are concerned. Some international bodies exist which are relatively generic in
nature, such as the World Travel and Tourism Council, while others have more
specific areas of concern, such as the International Hotels Environment Initiative
(International Hotels Environment Initiative, 1994).

Advice from trade associations and other bodies also exists at the national
level. The British Holiday and Home Parks Association, for example, has adopted
an environmental code to provide guidelines for operators in its sector, these
guidelines being based on sustainable tourism principles created by the UK government as part of its 'Tourism and the environment – maintaining the balance'
initiative (English Tourist Board, 1991). Codes of practice and other guidelines are
now available for virtually all sizes and types of operators within the tourism and
recreation industry.

Finally, and perhaps most significant of all, are the collaborations between
industry and governmental organizations. At the international level, for example,
the World Travel and Tourism Council and the World Tourism Organisation,
working together with the Earth Council, produced guidelines on Agenda 21 for
the travel and tourism industry (WTTC/WTO/Earth Council, 1995). Many examples also exist at the national level; in the UK, for example, the Institute of Leisure
and Amenity Management has worked with English Nature and the Pesticides
Trust to develop the Green Flag award denoting public parks of excellence.

One of the key principles recognized in Agenda 21 is that co-operation
between different stakeholder groups in society is necessary if progress on sustainable development is to be made.

Sustainable business management: the implications

The environment as an issue creates both opportunities and constraints for
tourism and recreation. The aim of sustaining environmental quality has grown
in importance and is likely to continue to do so. It is clear that a truly sustainable
pattern of development, however that may be defined, is far from being achieved
at present. Most of what needs to be done still remains to be done, and to a large
extent the onus is on companies, who are expected to play a major role in placing
society on a more sustainable footing.

The need for companies to improve their environmental performance is
inescapable, both in terms of protecting the environment and ensuring their own
long-term survival. The issue from a business point of view requires management.
This is particularly imperative in the tourism and recreation industry, which in so
many ways relies on environmental quality as an indispensable asset. Some of the
strategic considerations for companies are examined in the following section.

Long-termism

By its very nature, sustainable development necessitates taking a long-term view
when decisions are being made. The political and legal framework at all levels

increasingly reflects this approach, and so company policies should similarly adopt the principle that environmental assets should be managed in a sustainable fashion as opposed to being exploited destructively for short-term gain.

Responsibility

Companies were once able to operate in ways that reflected a ruthless and relentless drive for profits with few responsibilities to take into consideration, other than to themselves and their shareholders. There is now growing expectation, however, that companies should demonstrate responsible attitudes and be held accountable for their actions and any problems they may cause. Where tourism is concerned, for example, it is expected that operators demonstrate responsibility towards destination environments, host communities and, of course, the visitor.

Partnership

It is increasingly difficult for companies working alone to adequately meet the full range of stakeholder expectations. Co-operation and collaboration with relevant partners are necessary in order to achieve harmony between the social, economic and environmental aims of sustainable development. Partnership approaches are proving to be effective and mutually beneficial for those involved. In the rural context, for example, the Countryside Commission (1995) provides many useful examples of partnerships aimed at sustainable tourism which are helping to create social, economic and environmental benefits.

Efficiency

The policy and legal framework within which the tourism and recreation industry operates will increasingly dictate against excessive consumption of materials and water, high energy consumption, polluting emissions and discharges, and waste generation. The 'polluter pays' principle will necessitate that environmental costs arising from business activity be paid by those enterprises responsible.

Production issues

The production of goods and services often creates discernible environmental effects, but if environmental issues are to be adequately dealt with, those effects that are indirect and less obvious (though not necessarily less important) also need to be taken into account. This holistic view of the environmental effects of companies has led to the use of life-cycle assessment (LCA) in manufacturing industries. LCA assesses the environmental effects created at all stages of a product's life, from the procurement of raw materials through to production, distribution, use and disposal.

A recent development has seen the application of the LCA approach to tourism and recreation. Studies by British Airways Holidays, for example, have examined the impacts of tourism on the Seychelles and St Lucia. Various aspects of the holiday product, such as transport, resource use and infrastructure operation were assessed in terms of the scale of their contribution to the likes of air and water pollution, resource consumption and habitat loss (British Airways, 1996; British Airways,1998). Other examples exist of this approach being applied, especially where the construction and operation of hotels are concerned (Perera, 1997).

Openness

Stakeholder groups of various kinds, including the general public, have a legitimate interest in the environmental performance of companies. The overarching legal and policy framework increasingly demands that information about environmental performance is made available and that companies should move towards internalizing their environmental costs. Consequently, corporate environmental reporting is a growth area of activity, particularly among large companies, and many such reports are beginning to acknowledge, quantify and evaluate the burdens placed on the environment by the companies concerned.

Proactivity

Alongside an ever-more demanding legal framework governing standards of environmental performance, companies are also faced with a growing range of economic and market-based incentives which are designed to encourage and reward improvements in environmental performance. Given the existence of such a framework, it is clearly in a company's best interests to adopt a proactive approach by willingly improving its environmental performance in order to increase its potential for exploiting the cost-cutting and profit-enhancing benefits that are offered.

In line with this approach, the voluntary adoption of relevant sector guidelines and participation in available award and certification schemes are among the many initiatives that could be taken by companies to strengthen their position and validate their activities in the eyes of stakeholders.

Integration

The emergence of sustainable development as an objective for society acknowledges that all human activities impact upon the environment to a greater or lesser degree, a fact that is certainly evident where companies and their activities are concerned. It is increasingly expected that companies should consider the environmental implications of all their major activities and address their environmental performance accordingly. Delivering improvements in environmental performance should be an integral part of the management aims of the organization.

The environment as a management issue should be incorporated into existing management systems of the company. Rather than necessitate the creation of an additional and entirely new management structure, recognized environmental management system standards such as ISO 14001 are intended to complement conventional management approaches to issues such as quality and health and safety. The fact that the principles embodied in a sound environmental management system are in accord with existing, commonly applied management principles within organizations makes the adoption of such a system more straightforward and allows its aims to complement the overall performance aims of the company.

Summary

As the global human population continues its rapid growth and, by necessity, human exploitation of environmental resources continues to expand, it will become ever more imperative that the environment is managed in such a way as to allow it to continue to meet our needs. Environmental management is increasingly seen as the responsibility of all sectors of society: as a major consumer of environmental resources and contributor to environmental impacts, the tourism and recreation sector must play its part.

Chapter 3

Environmental Management of Tourism and Recreation at the Local Level

Objectives

The objectives of this chapter are to:

- summarize the nature of tourism in the countryside;
- examine both the positive and negative environmental impacts that can be attributed to tourism in the countryside;
- outline sustainability as a countryside tourism management aim;
- describe sustainable tourism in the countryside at a micro level;
- examine management actions to be implemented at the local level to meet the management aim of sustainable tourism.

Introduction

The last three decades have seen a dramatic growth of participation in countryside tourism. This has resulted in a considerable increase in the volume of people demanding access to the countryside (Green, 1981; Valentine, 1991; Lascelles, 1995). Growth in participation has brought with it a concern for the negative environmental impacts that can be attributed to countryside tourism, but also the hope that the countryside will prosper from the positive environmental impacts (English Tourist Board, 1991).

The previous chapter, by focusing on environmental issues for tourism and recreation at a macro level, has established the context. This chapter examines micro-level management actions that can ensure that the negative environmental impacts are minimized while the positive environmental impacts are encouraged. The structure of the chapter is as follows. First, tourism in the countryside is summarized and the potential impacts examined. Second, a symbiotic relationship is proposed between the countryside and tourism. Third, the concept of sustainable tourism is introduced as an overall management aim for countryside tourism operators. Fourth, the chapter proposes management actions that can be implemented by operators at the local level to progress towards sustainable tourism.

The nature of tourism in the countryside

The countryside is a resource that has diverse characteristics. The term 'country-side' is used to describe landforms and land uses but is as dependent on individual perceptions and experiences as it is on the physical or geographical characteristics of the land (Sharpley, 1996). The types of tourism in the countryside are also diverse. An ever-increasing variety of outdoor recreation activities have meant that the boundaries set by traditional definitions become hard to work within. Yet if we see each of the countryside's characteristics, be they accommodation types, historic or cultural aspects or a river or forest as no more than a physical setting, then countryside tourism becomes recreation activities that take place in these physical settings. However, it is important to note that as the variety of outdoor recreation activities increase so does the potential for new environmental impacts. Therefore the challenge is for the many operators charged with the promotion, control and facilitation of these recreation activities, new or old, to demonstrate concern and respond to the environmental impacts, both negative and positive, placed upon the physical setting that they manage.

The environmental impacts of countryside tourism

As demand grows for countryside tourism, opportunities for visitors to take part in the recreation activities of their choice are provided through the development of physical settings. Economic and employment benefits that may arise are often cited as justification for this development. Job creation is of significant impor-tance in the countryside as job losses in traditional rural industries have occurred. However, with the increasing variety of recreation activities, traditional industries can become physical settings for recreation activities themselves.

When fishing alone can no longer support the local com-munity, new employment opportunities generated by tourism may be welcomed. Here a fisher-man takes a group of tourists to ride the rapids

A local crafts-man who uses produce from the Forest of Mercia to produce furni-ture both for the forest and to sell externally

A miner's chair· locally produced in the Forest of Mercia to reflect local culture

Unlike most industries where a product is delivered to its market, with countryside tourism the market travels to the product (Hunter and Green, 1995). Remoteness, which makes many businesses uneconomical, can therefore become a market opportunity. This means that with the provision of recreation activities in the countryside, the potential exists to create and, perhaps more importantly, retain jobs. First, direct employment can be created at the physical setting itself or in nearby accommodation outlets. Second, jobs may also be retained throughout the service sector surrounding the physical setting as visitors use local shops, facilities and public transport. Case Study 3.1 illustrates how the construction and operation of the three English Center Parcs holiday villages has boosted the local economy and created employment opportunities.

Social benefits are often closely associated with economic benefits as they are concerned with quality of life. Although individual perceptions need to be accounted for, an increase and thus a wider diversity of recreation opportunities such as attractions, shops and public services have the potential to improve the quality of life of a local community.

As well as tourism providing social and economic benefits to local communities, it can also be responsible for improving the physical environment. Although visitors can be attracted to a physical setting because of the recreation activities that are available, the attractiveness of the physical setting is also a significant factor. If tourism is seen positively by the local community and benefits trickle through to

---

CASE STUDY 3.1

The economic impact of Center Parcs on local economies

Center Parcs have three sites in England that occupy over 400 acres of woodland situated in the countryside. The three sites represent the largest development of its kind within England's countryside. The economic activity generated by the three sites provides a considerable potential for job generation.

The Rural Development Commission (now the Countryside Agency) produced a report on the economic impact of Holiday Villages. This breaks the economic effects of each Center Parcs village into four parts:

1. Jobs created by the construction of holiday villages

It was calculated that out of the total construction cost of each new village approximately £22 million represents expenditure in the local area generating a one-off impact of £12 million in local income and the equivalent of 900 job years.

2. The operation of a holiday village

Over 100 jobs are generated in each village providing an injection of more than £7 million per year in wages and salaries into the local economy.

3. Purchases

Over 50 per cent of the supplies and services necessary to operate each village are purchased from local producers and suppliers and local depots of national suppliers. 140 extra jobs are generated in those local businesses directly supplying Center Parcs

4. Visitor expenditure off-site

The research showed that over 70 per cent of visitors to Center Parcs villages are first-time visitors who therefore wish to explore the surrounding area. Other tourism attractions around the villages have benefited as a direct result of Center Parcs' presence.

Source: Gratton (1997)

Tourists travelling down the river have provided the motivation to restore this traditional Finnish smoke sauna

them, the likelihood is that they will fashion the physical setting that they live in to attract more visitors and potentially create more positive environmental impacts. The built environment can also prosper. Tourism and recreation often provide the motivation for restoring derelict buildings, and many existing historical buildings in the countryside rely on the income generated from visitors to survive.

Whilst with sympathetic management tourism and recreation can result in positive environmental impacts, there is always the threat of negative environmental impacts occurring. These negative environmental impacts are most visible at those physical settings that attract large amounts of visitors. Over recent years concern has mounted over damage to particular physical settings caused by sheer numbers of visitors (Environment Committee, 1995).

Ceballos-Lascurain (1996:55) states: 'Overcrowding, misuse of natural resources, the construction of buildings and infrastructure, and other activities associated with tourism, produce impacts on the environment'. The actual negative environmental impacts of tourism will vary according to the number of visitors, the recreation activity that they partake in and the characteristics of the physical setting. Negative environmental impacts represent a major management problem. Ceballos-Lascurain (*idem*) notes that 'as with most problems, the negative impacts of tourism can only be managed effectively if they have been identified, measured and evaluated'. This implies that management of negative impacts is mainly reactive. Although difficult, proactive management of negative environmental impacts is required if they are to be avoided rather than just reduced.

When examining negative environmental impacts, they generally fall into the two categories of either physical impacts or social/cultural impacts (Sharpley, 1996). It is the physical impacts that are easiest to identify as the social/cultural impacts rely heavily on individual perception. Physical impacts include erosion, physical pollution, noise pollution, aesthetic pollution, soil damage, vegetation damage and wildlife disturbance, and all have an effect on the physical environment of the countryside. Social/cultural impacts are not so easy to classify as they do not leave a physical trace but instead affect those who live in and use a physical setting. They include conflict between visitors, conflict between visitors and the local community, crowding and congestion. Tourism is an amalgam of inter-linked recreation activities and it is often difficult to distinguish environmental impacts arising from individual recreation activities (Ceballos-Lascurain, 1996). Eventually all negative environmental impacts will not only devalue the physical setting but also the visitor experience. Table 3.1 lists the major potential impacts of tourism on the environment – both positive and negative.

Table 3.1   Potential impacts of tourism

Negative impact	Potential problems
Changes in flora and fauna	• Disruption of breeding habits • Killing animals though hunting • Killing of animals in order to supply goods for the souvenir trade • Inward or outward migration of animals • Trampling and damage of vegetation by feet and vehicles • Destruction of vegetation through the gathering of wood or plants • Change in extent and/or nature of vegetation cover through clearance or planting to accommodate tourist amenities
Pollution	• Water pollution through discharges of sewage, spillages of oil/petrol • Air pollution from vehicle emissions, combustion of fuels for heating and lighting tourist amenities • Noise pollution from tourist transportation and activities
Erosion	• Compaction of soils causing increased surface run-off and erosion • Change in risk of occurrence of landslips/slides • Change in risk of avalanche occurrence • Damage to geological features • Damage to river banks
Natural resources	• Depletion of ground and surface water supplies • Depletion of fossil fuels to generate energy for tourist activity • Change in risk of occurrence of fire • Depletion of mineral resources for building materials • Over-exploitation of biological resources • Change in hydrological patterns • Change in land used for primary production
Waste materials	• Production of visitor waste • Production of amenity and general waste
Visual impact	• Amenities • Litter • Sewage
Positive impacts	Potential benefits
Economic	• Increased revenue • Direct employment • Indirect employment
Physical	• Beautification of the natural environment • Restoration of derelict buildings • Survival of historical buildings
Social	• Increased diversity of leisure activities • Increased services

Source: Adapted from Hunter and Green (1995)

Tourism and the countryside: a symbiotic relationship

Budowski (1976) was the first to identify a two-way interaction or, as he called it, symbiosis, between conservation and tourism and the possible way in which each can derive benefits from the other. His ideas were initially directed at nature conservation but have been used in Figure 3.1 to highlight a possible symbiotic relationship between the countryside and tourism.

As visitor numbers rise and the provision for visitors increases, this may encourage greater visitor numbers, which in turn increases pressure on the

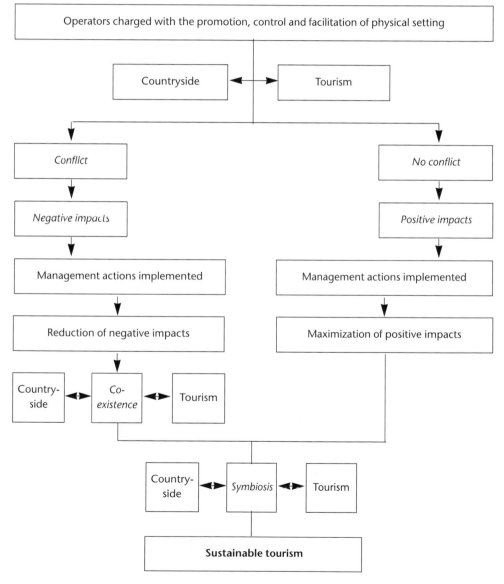

Figure 3.1 Tourism and the countryside: a symbiotic relationship

physical setting and magnifies the chances of conflict (negative environmental impacts) occurring between the resource (the countryside) and the product (tourism). As indicated in Figure 3.1 there may be aspects of tourism that cause no conflict at the physical setting but result in only positive environmental impacts. However this is rare, and the likelihood is that operators will need to implement reactive management actions to reduce negative environmental impacts. In reducing negative environmental impacts, tourism will be less detrimental to the countryside and therefore the two variables may become mutually tolerant of each other and coexist.

For the two variables to progress from simply coexisting to a desired symbiotic state, not only do the negative environmental impacts need to be reduced, but the positive environmental impacts maximized. Therefore proactive management actions need to be implemented to ensure this. To create the optimum symbiotic relationship both the countryside and tourism must derive benefits from each other's existence. It is the positive environmental impacts that can provide these necessary benefits. If a symbiotic relationship was found it would allow an increasing number of people to gain benefits from the countryside, be these physical, aesthetic, recreational, scientific or educational. At the same time the countryside and the people who live there would not suffer from tourism, but capitalize on its positive aspects. In other words, if a symbiotic relationship could be promoted, countryside tourism would become environmentally responsible and fulfil the management aim of sustainable tourism.

Sustainable tourism

The concept of sustainable development results from the observation that current generations are imposing too great of a demand upon the natural environment to allow it to continue to reproduce and maintain itself at its previous level of stability (Butler, 1998). The principle of sustainable development has been applied to tourism. Sustainable tourism therefore refers to tourism that is developed and managed in line with the principles of sustainable development (Hunter and Green, 1995).

These principles of sustainable development are primarily based on the theory of carrying capacity (FNNPE, 1993). Although originally a wildlife ecology term, carrying capacity has been applied to humans and, more specifically, to tourism visitors. It has been defined for the purpose of tourism as 'The maximum number of people who can use a site without an unacceptable alteration in the physical environment and without an unacceptable decline in the quality of the experience gained by visitors' (Mathieson and Wall, 1982). This definition implies that tourism carrying capacity is concerned with only two components: the quality of the environment and the quality of the recreation experience. Pritchard (1992), in clarifying their understanding of carrying capacity, add to Mathieson's and Wall's definition by stating that carrying capacity is also concerned with the social and psychological capacity of the physical setting to support tourist activity and development. In addition McIntyre and Hetherington (1991) include reference to the ability of the local community, economy and culture to support tourist activity in their explanation of tourism carrying capacity. From a definition that contained two variables we now have seven that bring with them a complexity that makes it difficult to accurately measure the actual carrying capacity of a physical setting. It is therefore of no surprise when Ceballos-Lascurain (1996: 136) states 'Actual carrying capacity can be a judgement call as to the acceptable level of change, both in terms of the resource and the satisfaction level of the visitors and the local community.'

In reality the calculation of carrying capacity relies as much on human values as resource and activity questions, and therefore is often subjective in nature. Wight (1998: 78) emphasizes this when stating: 'Unfortunately, carrying capacity as a guiding concept has limited success outside the field of wildlife management and cannot deal with the complexity and diversity of issues associated with tourism.' However, carrying capacity is one of the central theories behind the concept of sustainable development and so should not be ignored. Using carrying capacity theory in countryside tourism provides a useful way of thinking, as it focuses attention on the fact that there is a capacity which determines how much tourism growth the countryside can support, and that once this capacity is exceeded negative environmental impacts will occur. The calculation of a physical setting's carrying capacity is a complex task, susceptible to many variables. However difficult the calculation, a so-called 'magic number' of visitors that the physical setting can sustain will establish a benchmark that management actions can ensure is not exceeded.

Identifying an overall approach to the management of countryside tourism, such as the concept of sustainable tourism, can provide principles for operators to work within. However, theorizing about sustainable tourism alone is not adequate. Fundamental for operators at a local level, if these theories are to be turned into sustainable practical achievements, is the need to first realize that management action is required, and second to know what management action can be taken. Wight (1998: 75) recognizes this when she states: 'While sustainable tourism principles are well articulated, the "how's" are less frequently discussed. Theorising is useful, but tourism professionals need practical tools to implement some of the new approaches.' Butler (1998: 27) adds: 'The adoption of the principles of development to tourism has been rapid and widespread, although implementation of the practice has been much more limited.'

Hunter and Green (1995: 89) note that 'many operators remain comparatively ignorant of the potential impacts of tourism on the environment and the long-term reliance of tourism success on the maintenance of high environmental quality'. Therefore the remainder of this chapter is based on management actions that can be taken at the local level in order to support sustainable tourism. Although common approaches can be established, it is important to recognize that there are no universal solutions, as management actions must be tailored to the particular characteristics of each physical setting, the visitors and the recreational activities that take place there.

Management actions

Negative environmental impacts of tourism arise through the construction and operation of visitor amenities or services and from the recreation activities of the visitors themselves (Hunter and Green, 1995). Management actions may be divided into the following types:

- visitor management to reduce visitor impact on the physical setting;
- amenity management to reduce the amenity impact on the physical setting;
- management actions to reduce the off-site impacts of running the physical setting;
- management actions to maximize the contribution of tourism and recreation to the local economy.

Each of these is now considered in turn.

Visitor management: reducing visitor impact on the physical setting

The overall aim of visitor management is to minimize the negative impacts of tourism on the environment while simultaneously enhancing visitor experience. Visitor management as a management technique covers a wide range of actions that, according to Jim (1989), fall into three categories. These are:

1. influencing visitor behaviour;
2. redistributing use;
3. rationing use.

Influencing visitor behaviour

Jim's first visitor management technique is influencing visitor behaviour. If visitor behaviour can be influenced, negative environmental impacts can be prevented before they occur. Five methods of influencing the behaviour of visitors are highlighted. These are education, interpretation, codes of conduct, controlling visitors, and marketing of the physical setting according to its capacities.

Negative environmental impacts may arise from the selfish or thoughtless behaviour of visitors. This may be due in some cases to visitors simply not being aware of the potentially harmful negative environmental impacts of their recreation activities. Therefore visitors should be educated in issues of sustainability so that they do not detrimentally affect the experience of others and so that they will get the most out of their own experience. An educational campaign and the information it contains needs to have clear focus. Whatever the method utilized, it is critical that it is presented in a style that visitors can enjoy, understand and then act upon. Perhaps the best educational campaign is a pre-visit. If visitors are advised how to behave before arriving at the physical setting, empathy for the environment and the site can be created. Case Study 3.2 highlights an example of an effort to instil into schoolchildren empathy for trees, woodlands, the forestry industry and the timber trade.

CASE STUDY 3.2

The Forest Education Initiative

The Forest Education Initiative (FEI) brings together people who grow and use timber with those who work in education. It aims to increase young people's understanding of the local and global importance of trees, woodlands, the forestry industry and the timber trade, and links between them.

FEI cluster groups are being developed throughout Britain. These local clusters bring together teachers, foresters, timber processors and manufacturers who provide local information and resources for schools. They may hold teachers' workshops and enable schools to organize first-hand learning experiences for pupils in local woods, paper and saw mills, and factories.

The FEI teaching packs help young people to make connections between sustainable multi-purpose woodlands and how wood is used. Three new illustrated books, written by teachers, suggest activities to explore forestry, timber processing and products; trade and international development; recreation, conservation and economic issues in today's woods and forests, both locally and globally. The books are:

- *Only Made of Wood*: A resource designed for 5-to-7-year-olds. It consists of a beautifully illustrated story-

book and a photocopiable teacher's book packed with ideas for indoor and outdoor activities. Includes curriculum references and costs £11.90, plus £1.25 p&p, and can be obtained from Biblios PDS Ltd, Star Road, Partridge Green, West Sussex, RH13 8LD.

- *The Wonder of Wood*: An activity based resource for 7-to-11-year-olds. Silva the owl encourages children to look at trees and the uses of wood locally and in other parts of the world. Guidelines link the activities to the National Curriculum Key Stage 2. The pack costs £9.50 and can be obtained from the FEI co-ordinator, Margaret Hardy.

- *Investigating Trees and Timber*: Designed to allow secondary pupils to explore the role of timber in our lives. Aimed at 14-to-16-year-olds it has links with Geography, Science, Technology, Business Studies and PSE. The cost of the pack is £11.50 and can be obtained from the FEI co-ordinator, Margaret Hardy.

Source: Yarrow (1998).

For further information contact: The Co-ordinator, Margaret Hardy, Great Eastern House, Tension Road, Cambridge, CB1 2DU

Another management action that can help instil empathy in visitors is interpretation. Tilden (1957) suggests that 'interpretation is about instilling empathy for the subject by revealing to visitors something of the beauty and wonder, the inspiration and spiritual meaning that lie behind what the visitor can with his senses perceive'. Aldridge (1975) explains interpretation simply as 'the art of explaining the character of an area'. Herbert (1989) states: 'Interpretation has a dual purpose of preserving the best interests of the visitors and the place they visit.'

Sustainability can be interpreted throughout the physical setting to provide a learning experience using observation and participation. Interpretation techniques include guided walks, self-directed walks, nature trails, panels, plaques and literature. The key to successful interpretation is to match the style of interpretation to the type of visitor. Case Study 3.3 gives an example of how interpretation can be designed with the regular visitor in mind, and without excessive expense.

CASE STUDY 3.3

Hanging out in the woods: a cheap and effective form of interpretation

Providing the visitor with permanent and high-quality interpretative material, so they can learn more about forests, can be very expensive, particularly if the operator is expected to foot all or part of the bill.

There are a number of organizations and commercial enterprises that cater for owners' and managers' needs in providing ready-made signs, pictorial boards and way-markers. However, like the people visiting them, forests come in a variety of types and sizes. All too often interpretation material is not site-specific and does not cater for the type of visitor attracted. If a forest is small it is likely to attract a regular clientele of local people. If this is the case, high-profile and costly fixed display panels may not be the best educational or financial method.

The Royal Forestry Society's Hockeridge and Pancake Woods on the Chilterns practise multi-purpose sustainable management which incorporates natural conservation, landscape enhancement, informal recreation and public education and awareness. The woods attract regular visitors who know the woodlands and their footpath networks well.

Due to a small budget, it was decided that an alternative to permanent interpretative methods would be sought. The management team came up with easy-to-read, home-made notices, containing only three or four paragraphs of interpretative information. These notices were produced on a word processor, printed on to brightly coloured A4 paper and laminated to make them waterproof. During the manager's routine inspections these notices are hung at appropriate points throughout the woods. Hanging the notices removes the need for expensive mountings and has proved to be a cheap and effective display method. The notices are used to highlight woodland management practices, sensitive areas and seasonal attractions.

The possibilities are endless and a bank of new and reusable notices is being built up. Care has been taken to make the notices appealing to visitors with different levels of environmental awareness. Connections with folklore, history and medicinal uses help to achieve this.

The notices are designed to disseminate forestry practice and terminology, influence visitor behaviour and reassure them that the woods are in good hands. There are many woods, similar to Hockeridge and Pancake, which are primarily working woods but attempt to provide a multitude of other benefits for all. Where the bulk of visitors are regulars, and budgets are tight, the Royal Forestry Society has shown that there can be an effective alternative to permanent interpretative material.

Source: Royal Forestry Society, 102 High Street, Tring, Hertfordshire, HP23 4AH

Codes of conduct are designed to change the way visitors act. They should be a simple and clearly understandable list of recommendations designed to reduce negative and encourage positive environmental impacts. A well-known code of conduct is the 'Country Code' (UK) from 1953. It is general in its approach, concentrating on visitor behaviour on agricultural land. Sharpley (1996: 278) points out that 'although 75 per cent of visitors to the countryside can recall at least one of its points it does very little to raise visitors' awareness of the broader issues related to the sustainable use of the countryside as a resource for recreation'. In suggesting how visitors should behave, codes of conduct have the potential to encourage positive environmental impacts. The Countryside Commission's *Guide for the Green Tourist* (1991) fulfils this potential by giving consideration to the off-site impacts of running the physical setting and the contribution of site activities to the local economy. It is reproduced in Figure 3.2.

- Consider the effect of your visit wherever you travel – at home, abroad and especially in the world's most beautiful places.
- Take time to learn in advance about the place you are going to visit.
- Wherever possible, stay in small-scale, locally owned accommodation.
- Show friendship, respect local custom and lifestyles, support skills, services and produce.
- Whenever possible, travel by your own muscle power – on foot or cycle – or use public transport.
- Spend sufficient time in an area to get to know and understand it.
- Support the conservation of natural beauty throughout the world.

Figure 3.2 Countryside Commission's Guide for Green Tourists. *Source: Countryside Commission (1991)*

As the variety of outdoor recreation activities available to visitors to the countryside has increased, so has the potential for negative environmental impacts. Specific codes of conduct have been introduced for individual recreation activities. These include those recreation activities that are not traditionally seen as suitable for the countryside. Off-road driving is one such activity, which has had a code of conduct written as an attempt to limit its impact on the environment. This is highlighted in Case Study 3.4.

Although a code of conduct is flexible in that it can contain guidelines for generic, site-specific or activity-specific behaviour, they have one major drawback. This, according to Sharpley (1996: 280), is that 'the degree to which they are adhered to is totally dependent on the willingness of individual visitors to adapt their behaviour and their ability to accept responsibility for the environment'.

Management actions can be used to concentrate visitors rather than allow them to disperse freely throughout a site. Clearly marked footpaths, strategically placed visitor facilities and information points will tend to concentrate visitors and give some control over what they do and where they do it. In this way visitors can be subtly moved away from areas of the physical setting that are susceptible to

CASE STUDY 3.4

The Department of Conservation and Land Management (CALM): 4 × 4 driving ethics

CALM is the State Government agency responsible for the management of Western Australia's national parks, conservation parks, marine parks, state forests and timber reserves, nature reserves, marine nature reserves, and all associated forest produce, native plants and animals. They are also responsible for conserving native plants and animals throughout the state and managing their sustainable use.

CALM has several responsibilities, which are carefully integrated. They manage lands and waters for their renewable resources, for the recreation and tourism they can support, and for the conservation of the native wildlife, both plant and animal, which they sustain. CALM's primary responsibility is to manage these lands and waters on an ecologically sustainable basis, so that the needs of the present are met without compromising the choices of future generations.

Each year, more and more people are discovering that the best way to experience Western Australia is to pack up their four-wheel drive and head off to the forest. Like other outdoor recreationists, four-wheel drive vehicle owners and drivers who access public lands have a responsibility or 'duty of care' to help protect Western Australia's flora, fauna and natural landscapes so that future generations of users will be able to enjoy what we now take for granted.

The Australian National Four Wheel Drive Council has developed a Four-Wheel Driver's Code of Ethics, to help minimize negative environmental impacts. The code's twelve points are:

1. Keep to the laws and regulations for 4WD vehicles.
2. Keep to constructed vehicle tracks. Do not drive 'off-road' except in permitted areas.
3. Keep the environment clean. Carry your own rubbish home.
4. Obey restrictions on the use of public lands. Respect national parks and other conservation areas.
5. Obtain permission before driving on private land. Leave livestock alone and gates as found.
6. Keep your vehicle mechanically sound.
7. Take adequate water, food, fuel and spares on trips. In remote areas, travel with another vehicle.
8. Respect our wildlife. Stop and look, but never disturb or chase animals.
9. Respect other recreation users' rights to peace and solitude in the bush.
10. Obey all fire restrictions. Extinguish your fire before leaving. Don't let your exhaust emit sparks.
11. Help in bushfire emergencies and search and rescue, if you are properly equipped and able.
12. Join a 4WD club and support 4WD touring as a responsible and legitimate recreational activity.

negative impacts such as erosion and soil damage. Concentration has to take place without making visitors feel crowded, and therefore a level of compromise needs to be found or negative social/cultural impacts such as crowding and conflict between users may occur.

Marketing can be used not only to attract more visitors, but also affect the kind of visitors that are attracted, and in doing so match visitors to the site's characteristics. Visits to the countryside are seasonal by nature. It is at the peak times of demand that greatest pressure is placed on the physical setting and the potential for negative environmental impacts rises. Marketing can be used to reduce seasonal variations in demand through the promotion of out-of-season visits. It is also possible to use de-marketing as a management action, by, for example, removing the site from tourist maps, brochures and information centres to reduce demand if pressure levels are too great.

Redistributing visitor use

Jim's (1989) second visitor management technique is redistributing visitor use. The primary purpose of redistributing visitor use is to match recreational demand with the carrying capacity of the physical setting. This approach is commonly used when a physical setting's carrying capacity is or is near to being exceeded. To redistribute visitor use it is necessary to understand the compatibility of different recreation activities and the principles of zoning.

An operator needs to focus on two areas of compatibility. First the compatibility of the physical setting with the recreation activities that take place there. Negative environmental impacts can occur at a physical setting if a recreation activity takes place on land that is not intended for that specific recreation activity. Second there is the compatibility of different recreation activities themselves. Recreation activities are not always compatible. For example noisy activities are incompatible with those activities that depend on peaceful countryside locations.

The more intensive the use of a physical setting, the less likely it is that another activity can take place at the same time or in the same place. For example competitive events will usually require sole use of a physical setting. Informal and casual recreation may be compatible but much depends on the skill of the participant, for example ability to control a horse on a busy footpath or keep a canoe from becoming tangled in anglers' lines (Goodall and Whittow, 1975). To solve the issue of compatibility it may be necessary to take zoning action.

Zoning will be necessary where incompatibility exists between either different types of recreation activities or a recreation activity and the natural environment. It may involve the exclusion of one or more recreation activities from a particular area of the physical setting. Zoning can also be used to match recreation activities with suitable areas of land, to allow sensitive areas of land to be left alone or regenerate if damaged. It is possible to zone by *space* or *time*.

Space zoning is the direction of activities to use specific areas. This is required either because activities are incompatible or the natural environment is not tolerant of certain or all activities. It designates particular areas of a site for specific uses and it redistributes and manages demand by separating recreational activities according to the capacity and character of the landscape and the need for conservation or regeneration. Case Study 3.5 highlights how the Whakarewarewa Forest in Rotorua (New Zealand) has been space zoned.

CASE STUDY 3.5

Space zoning – keeping everyone happy

Many forests cater to a wide range of visitors, who come to the forest for a variety of reasons. The limited amount of space can lead to visitors participating in different activities coming into conflict with each other. Trying to reconcile the needs of these different visitor groups – walkers, horse riders and mountain bikers – is proving a management challenge around the world.

There is one setting – the forest – which can cater to many different types of activities. The activity in which visitors take part is determined by the experience that they would like to have. Other visitors doing different activities in the same area may compromise this experience.

The Whakarewarewa Forest in Rotorua, New Zealand has used space-zoning action to try and enable visitors to achieve their desired experience. The forest is located on the edge of Rotorua, five minutes' drive from the city centre and as such is easily accessible to a wide variety of users – families, individuals, locals and visitors to the area. The 5,667 hectare forest is managed by Fletcher Challenge Forests as a multipurpose, sustainable commercial forest with specific areas set aside for recreational use. The recreational uses of the forest include walking, running, horse riding, bird watching, orienteering, mountain biking and motocross riding.

In an attempt to avoid user conflict, the management has established dedicated tracks for specific activities, effectively space zoning the physical setting. There are walking tracks, horse riding tracks and mountain biking tracks. Some tracks are used by both horses and mountain bikes, but the majority are single use. Mountain bikers or horses must not use the dedicated walking tracks. The same goes for the dedicated mountain bike tracks, which are not to be used by walkers, runners or horses. The forest also caters to motocross riders, with a dedicated track for their use. The Visitor Centre provides information and maps on all the activities available in the forest, as well as educational material on plantation forestry. Once in the forest the tracks are clearly signposted, with colour markings and wooden signs indicating track use at the start of each track. There are no forest rangers to ensure compliance, but anecdotal evidence suggests that space zoning is working very well.

Source: Sarah Leberman, Department of Management Systems, Massey University, Palmerston North, New Zealand

Time zoning is the use of time limitation or seasonality to programme an activity's use of an area. It is likely to prove necessary where there is heavy pressure of demand from several recreational activities which all have similar site requirements. Case Study 3.6 illustrates how time zoning has been implemented in the Dunas de S. Jacinto Nature Reserve (Portugal), to provide a safe habitat for birds during the hunting season.

CASE STUDY 3.6

Time zoning activities

Site review

The Nature Reserve of Dunas de S. Jacinto is part of a Special Protection Area. It is a refuge to a great number of migratory birds, which use it as a sanctuary during the hunting season between the months of August and November. Monitoring studies have shown that birds fly into the reserve's protected dunes, pinewoods and stagnant ponds to escape the surrounding hunting areas.

Programme

The reserve's main objective is to provide a safe habitat for birds during the hunting season. Two types of actions were programmed by management staff to help this. Attention was first given to preserving and improving the birds' preferred natural habitat within the reserve. Second, attention was paid to maintaining compatibility between the reserve's recreation and education activities and its preservation and protection objectives.

Guided visits along a set route are the main recreation activity that takes place in the reserve. These visits are limited to thirty visitors at a time. It was a concern of man-agement that the presence of visitors in the reserve on hunting days could drive the birds away from the protection of the reserve and into the nearby hunting areas. It was decided to introduce a time zoning to redistribute visitor use. The principle of the action was that there would be no recreation activity on hunting days (Thursday, Sundays and holidays) to keep the site as quiet as possible.

Operations

When implementing the action it was extremely important to inform visitors of the environmental objective behind it. Information was disseminated through reserve leaflets and information boards located at the visitor centre and at the starting point of the set route.

Audit and review

The time zoning action has been monitored and the results are displayed in the visitor centre.

Source: Instituto da Conservação da Natureza – Delegação de Coimbra, Mata Nacional do Choupal, 3000 Coimbra, Portugal

Figure 3.3 highlights the varying compatibility of a selection of land-based recreation activities. Three situations regarding the degree of compatibility of the land uses are represented in the matrix. The matrix demonstrates how space and time zoning are directly connected to compatibility issues and how they can be used to alleviate conflict caused by incompatible recreation activities.

Rationing visitor use

The third of Jim's (1989) visitor management techniques is rationing visitor use. If a physical setting's carrying capacity is being exceeded it may be necessary to regulate the number of visitors allowed at any one time. If it is necessary to use any of the following rationing techniques, it is essential that the policy be clearly communicated to users to avoid resentment or dissatisfaction. Sharpley (1996) explains a number of rationing actions.

	Wildfowling	Golf	Motor sports	Mountain biking	Horse riding	Walking	Angling	Orienteering
Wildfowling								
Golf	✖							
Motor sports	✖	✖						
Mountain biking	✔	✖	✖					
Horse riding	✔	✔	✖	✔				
Walking	✔	✔	✖	✖	✔			
Angling	✖	✖	✖	✔	✔	♥		
Orienteering	✔	✖	✖	✔	✔	♥	✔	

Key:

♥ = **complete compatibility.** Activities could take place on an area of land at the same time.

✔ = **partial compatibility.** Activities could take place on an area of land, but at different times. Time zoning is required.

✖ = **incompatibility.** Activities could not take place on the same area of land. Space zoning is required.

Figure 3.3 The compatibility of selected land-based recreational activities. *Source: adapted from Goodall and Whittow (1975).*

Charging for use is a simple way of rationing. Here it may be necessary to experiment with different prices in order to equate visitor demand with carrying capacity. It may also be necessary to have a differential pricing structure to reduce demand at peak periods. Some organizations, such as the National Trust in the UK, incorporate free entry days so that those who cannot afford entry charges do not become excluded.

The issuing of time tickets can regulate visitors by permitting entry either at specific times or for a specific duration of time. The primary purpose of time ticketing is in assuring that the physical capacity of the physical setting is not exceeded. Time ticketing can achieve this by maintaining a regular and even flow of visitors. The principle is highlighted by Case Study 3.7.

For some recreation activities pre-booking is required. Entry to areas of special interest, in particular nature reserves and other protected areas, are often subject to obtaining permission. For group visits to a physical setting, prior notice may be required by the operator. This will help the management to plan necessary actions and in doing so reduce the possible negative environmental impacts.

Permits are an option for recreation operators with sensitive sites. Permits usually need to be applied for in advance and therefore can be issued selectively

CASE STUDY 3.7

National Trust time ticket scheme

Many National Trust properties are extremely popular, especially on public holidays and summer weekends. At some houses and gardens timed tickets may be issued to smooth the flow of people entering the property (but not the duration of the visit). All visitors, including National Trust members, are required to use these tickets. This system is designed to create better viewing conditions for visitors and to minimize wear and tear on historic house interiors and gardens.

No. GW.

WYTHAM WOODS

TEMPORARY PERMIT

.......Mr. R. Vickery........... *has permission to walk*

in Wytham Woods from 13 December '96. *to* 30 June '97.

.... NBMOTOCK.....

p *Land Agent to Oxford University.*

Please see rules printed overleaf

To gain access to Wytham Woods a permit is required. It is acquired by writing personally to the Land Agent at Oxford University. Permission to walk in the woods is granted to those whose reasons to enter the woods match the woods' policies.

and with an accompanying information package. This package can contain maps, educational guidance, rules and regulations, and even codes of conduct. This promotes self-education and responsibility from the recreationalist while at the same time allowing the operator to exercise control of visitor use through rationing.

The use of guided tours can limit the number of visitors in the physical setting at any one time, exercise control over behaviour, and provide a valuable source of education. This method can be especially effective for first-time visitors, and as a technique to influence future behaviour.

Prohibition of access to a physical setting may be required in exceptional circumstances to ration demand to highly sensitive areas or at specific times (for example breeding seasons for birds). Access can be denied to everyone or pinch points can be used to discriminate against users. There are many forms and styles of pinch points including concrete bollards, crocodile teeth, stiles, and logs. Pinch points are commonly found in car parks to stop cars leaving the designated parking areas. Logs can be used to obstruct pathways that the management does not want visitors to use.

A large log that matches the surroundings has been laid across the forest track to act as a pinch-point. It discriminates against users, stopping access by motor vehicle, but allowing pedestrians to pass by

Visitor management incurs costs but it may not be possible, practical or acceptable for operators to charge for entry to their physical setting. Case Study 3.8 illustrates an innovative way of raising funds developed through the Visitor Payback Project. The scheme offers a method of collecting funds for conservation work specifically but has the potential to be developed to cover broader environmental issues.

Amenity management: reducing the amenity impact on the physical setting

Visitor amenities, including centres, cafes, accommodation facilities, changing rooms, toilets and shops, are all common sights at physical settings in the countryside. Visitor amenities can be responsible for negative environmental impacts, but management action has the potential to reduce these and create positive environmental impacts. Sound environmental management of visitor amenities can create an attractive local area, encourage visitors to adopt environmentally sound practices both on and off site, persuade visitors to make positive decisions about local products and transport, and stimulate investment in the local economy. To maximize these positive environmental impacts, amenity management actions should be focused on making an efficient use of energy and water, and reducing, re-using and recycling waste.

Efficient use of energy and water

The reduction of both energy and water consumption at amenities is an important environmental aim. Reducing energy consumption will cut electricity and fuel bills and in doing so make a valuable contribution to the reduction of the burning of fossil fuels and the associated negative environmental impacts. Implementation of energy reduction schemes can be a relatively cheap and effective

CASE STUDY 3.8

Is it time for countryside visitors to 'pay back'?

In Sherwood Forest there is an 'Automatic Outlaw', who collects money for conservation issues and in return prints a sticker of one of Robin Hood's merry men.

Lack of money to sustain tourism destinations is a growing problem in Europe and across the world. As tourism continues to expand, many places are receiving more visitors without necessarily having sufficient resources to cope with the extra costs that this may entail. The physical settings that suffer the most are those that are freely accessible to the public and where entrance fees are either unpractical or unacceptable.

Today, the quality of the environment is an important consideration for visitors. This being so it is reasonable to expect that visitors will be prepared to pay to preserve what they themselves come to enjoy.

'Visitor Payback' is a term used to mean the process of visitors choosing to give money (or other help) to assist the conservation or management of places they visit. It is a term that refers to voluntary assistance. It offers a method of harnessing tourist-spending power, which can be linked directly to specific local conservation needs. It has the advantage of enabling visitors to understand the contribution that they are making. Similarly, tourism enterprises which participate feel that they are doing something practical to help their local environment. The 'Visitor Payback Project' explored this concept by establishing and monitoring five practical schemes in different European countries to establish what the best method of approaching visitors was. The results are summarized below.

Collection boxes. Donation boxes on their own collect very little. Passing a collection box around may bring far better results.

If this is thought to be inappropriate, collection boxes used in conjunction with display panels, posters and leaflets work well. Offering a small reward to donators such as a sticker, post card, certificate can boost contributions.

A single large payment. Visitors are asked to make a large payment to support a specific project in return for their name becoming associated with the project.

Subscriptions to a conservation club. Visitors are invited to join a club, which supports a conservation cause. Contribution is usually in the form of a subscription charge to encourage long-term commitment.

Additional payments. When visitors make a purchase, for example a T-shirt, food, or accommodation, they are asked to pay an additional amount towards a conservation cause. There are two types of additional payments. These are 'opt in' where visitors are asked to add an amount, and 'opt out' where a small amount is added to the bill and visitors pay it only if they wish to.

Events. Visitors attending free events are asked to voluntarily contribute to a conservation cause.

Conservation work. Rather than contributing directly, visitors are asked to assist in conservation work.

It was found that if a visitor payback scheme is to be effective the scheme should:

- make it easy for visitors to pay quickly;
- make sure clear instructions and well-chosen words are used to encourage visitors to pay;
- employ creative methods of collection and demonstrate enthusiasm when approaching visitors;
- have a clear conservation theme and be clear how and where visitors' money will be used.

Source: The Tourism Company, 3 The Homend, Ledbury, Herefordshire, HR8 1BN

Table 3.2 Savings from energy-efficient light bulbs

Standard bulb	Energy efficiency bulb	Approximate savings*
100 watt	20–23 watt	£39
75 watt	15–18 watt	£33
60 watt	11–13 watt	£27
40 watt	9 watt	£18

Savings* are based on 7.32 pence per kilowatt-hour tariff. By replacing a 100-watt bulb with a 23-watt energy efficient bulb, savings of £45 over the average life of an energy-efficient bulb, i.e. 8,000 hours, can be made. Subtracting from this the cost of the energy-efficient bulb (on average £10) less the cost of eight standard bulbs bought over the same period, bringing the total saving to £39.

Source: The Rural Development Commission (1996). The Green Audit Kit: A DIY guide to greening your tourism business. The Rural Development Commission, Bristol

way of cutting costs. For example, low energy light bulbs provide a simple way of reducing energy consumption. Table 3.2 shows the savings that can be made by switching to energy-efficient light bulbs.

Energy consumption can be reduced in a number of simple ways. First, low energy light bulbs require less electricity to produce the same amount of light as standard tungsten bulbs. This means they offer an effective way to save money while contributing to environmental aims. Energy efficient bulbs last eight times longer than normal tungsten bulbs, which justifies their extra cost. It is best practice to place these bulbs in places where light is required for long periods: it is in such places that savings will be most noticed.

Second, good insulation can help save energy consumption as it can reduce heating costs. Consideration should be given to insulating lofts, pipes, tanks and walls of amenity buildings. Double glazing reduces heat loss and thermostats regulate heating, and in doing so effectively lower heating bills by optimizing temperature settings for space and water heating.

Third, the energy efficiency of appliances should be considered. Over the lifetime of an appliance the cost of the energy to run it is likely to cost more than the appliance itself. For this reason, when a new appliance is purchased the amount of energy that it consumes should be an important consideration. Manufacturers display energy consumption levels on many new appliances. Appliance-operating times should be checked and appliances shut off when not in use, and it may be necessary to replace old, inefficient appliances with new, more efficient appliances. Case Study 3.9 illustrates how a Finnish Holiday Centre has implemented energy-saving actions, using a number of approaches.

It also makes environmental as well economic sense to conserve water. When purchasing washing machines and dishwashers, their water consumption can be as important as their energy consumption. With facilities like toilets, the advantages of a dual flush system should be considered, and a brick placed in the cistern is a practical, cheap and effective way of saving up to one litre of water with every flush.

Reducing, reusing and recycling waste

Tourism and recreation generate visitor waste and operator waste. There are a number of ways that waste generated by visitors can be managed. First, a 'No-bins, take your litter home' policy can be implemented. This may need to be backed up with an intense litter-collecting procedure to keep the physical setting clean.

Second, litter bins can be provided at focal points throughout the physical setting, such as the car park, shop, cafe, play and picnic areas. These bins need to be accompanied by separate bins for recycling purposes, and all bins need to be backed up by information as to where to find them. The location of bins should be marked on the physical setting map and information board. Case Study 3.10 shows how waste is dealt with in Ruunaa in Finland.

For an operator to successfully manage the waste that they themselves generate, a starting point is to identify the types generated and determine suitable

CASE STUDY 3.9

The environmental case of Huhmari Holiday Centre

The Huhmari Holiday Centre, North Karelia, is Finland's equivalent to Center Parcs. Situated in a coniferous forest by Lake Hoytiainen, the centre offers guests the choice of 87 villas and provides a main reception building which contains a restaurant, swimming pool and conference facilities.

In 1995 management commissioned Antti Kilpiainen, an environmentalist, to write an environmental plan for the centre. The plan was updated in 1997 to include the following five key areas:

1. Education of personnel.
2. Energy saving.
3. Recycling.
4. Protecting nature.
5. Increasing customers' knowledge about the environment.

The plan identifies impacts and proposes actions to reduce negative impacts and promote positive impacts. Energy consumption and waste disposal have been identified as the main issues.

The bulk of energy-saving actions are focused on the villas. Guests are provided with a switch which is located by the door giving them the opportunity to alternate the villa temperature between 17 degrees Celsius when going out and 22 degrees when inside. To save energy neither remote controls for television sets nor mini-bars are provided. Energy-saving bulbs are used in every light fitting and the heat that the air conditioning generates is recovered and used to heat the villas. Triple glazing and double doors help insulate the villas. The kitchen and restaurant areas conserve energy by limiting the use of dishwashers and using lower temperatures in the preparation of food where appropriate. The swimming pool is split into a hot and a cold area to reduce heating costs.

The Huhmari Holiday Centre does not have a municipal waste system at their disposal. Emphasis is therefore placed on the sorting of waste. Waste-disposal points offer the visitor the chance to separate waste into paper, glass, biodegradable and non-recyclable bins that the centre then delivers to the nearest recycling point. Although the holiday centre is located in a rural setting, negotiations with suppliers has meant that the delivery loads are consolidated where possible to reduce the number of lorries on local roads.

Source: Huhmari, 83700 Polvijarvi, Finland

---

methods of disposal. First the amount of waste generated should be reduced. Second, generated waste should be re-used whenever possible. For example composting the site's organic waste will mean that other waste can be left for longer periods without collection, as it will not rot. Compost can provide a free and effective garden fertilizer, as well as cutting the volume of waste that requires disposal. Third, waste should be recycled. Case Study 3.11 illustrates how waste water is recycled and then returned to watercourses in Portuguese recreation sites.

Packaging, especially plastic, can be one of the largest contributors of waste. Plastics are generally non-biodegradable and usually derive from a non-renewable source such as oil. Sensible purchasing can help to cut down on needless

CASE STUDY 3.10

Ruunaa waste service system, Finland

Cigarette butts cause a problem. Throwing them into litter bins increases the chance of fire. More usually they are stubbed out on the ground: this is visually polluting. The photograph illustrates an approach taken in Finland. Visitors are provided with small plastic cases in which to extinguish their cigarettes and then the cases can be safely thrown away

Ruunaa recreation centre was founded in 1987 and today attracts over 120,000 visitors a year. In 1997 these visitors generated 60m³ and in 1998 45m³ of waste. Waste management costs in 1998 were 40,000 Fmk.

The Finnish Forest and Park Service (FPS) aim to manage the area in an environmentally friendly way in accordance to their ISO 14001 certification. One objective of the FPS is to decrease the amount of waste created by visitors to the Ruunaa recreation area. Proposed actions include encouraging visitors to recycle waste and giving visitors more responsibility to manage their own waste.

Four ECO-points have been placed at rest-places that have shelters. These points have recycling containers for compost, bottles, cans, batteries, and a separate container for non-renewable waste. A shovel is provided for any materials that can be composted. Full instructions inform users of how to use the amenity and why they should use it. This information is written in Finnish but there are symbols to aid foreign users. Rest-places without shelters do not have anywhere to dispose or recycle waste. This has been done deliberately to encourage visitors to take their waste with them when they leave. ECO-points are clearly marked on guide maps if visitors do wish to recycle or dispose of waste.

Norske Veritas (a local company) monitors the effectiveness of the above actions in the form of an external audit. The audit is designed to provide information on the site's present operational state and highlights shortcomings. Any problems identified are addressed in the review of ISO 14001.

CASE STUDY 3.11

An environmental solution to waste-water treatment for recreational sites

An aquatic bed at Monsanto Ecological Park, Portugal

In Portugal a new system for waste-water treatment is being used for small urban areas or isolated houses with a total population of between 100 to 1,000 habitants. This system is referred to as an 'Aquatic Bed' and has the capability of being used in recreational sites as it has several advantages:

- It is aesthetically pleasant.
- It does not cause unpleasant smells.
- The waste water can be returned to watercourses without any damage.

The system consists of a small ground depression (or a small lagoon) with an artificial porous environment into which plants well adapted to aquatic life are planted.

Waste water is passed through the aquatic bed and is exposed to the porous plant roots. The plant roots purify the waste water, which becomes suitable to be returned to watercourses. For the best result, wastewater should receive a previous decant which, on small recreation sites, could occur in a septic pit or tank.

The majority of Portuguese aquatic beds have a superficial layer of grain laid on top of the local soil. These beds should have a little inclination (0.5 to 1 per cent) from entrance to exit point. This makes the process of drainage easier. The recommended bed plants are *Fragmites australis*, *Thypha latifolia* and *Scirpus lacustris*. These should be planted a distance of 25 to 30 cm apart from each other.

packaging and therefore on waste production. Operators should consider buying in bulk so that the products purchased come wrapped in only one layer of packaging instead of being individually wrapped. When products are passed or sold on to visitors, operators should try and avoid using a bag, but if a bag is necessary it should be paper as it is biodegradable and can be recycled efficiently.

Reducing the off-site impacts of operating the physical setting and maximizing benefits to the local community

Negative and positive environmental impacts also occur outside the physical setting because of the physical setting's existence. For example, visitors travelling to the physical setting may contribute to negative environmental impacts by using cars. Positive benefits may derive from a visitor's or operator's need to purchase goods from outside a physical setting's boundaries.

The private motor car

Effective transport management actions are essential in reducing the off-site environmental impacts caused by visitors to the physical setting. The private car often offers the visitor the most convenient method of reaching physical settings that are situated in the countryside, but it also has significant negative environmental impacts. The private motor car is a major contributor to pollution. According to Transport 2000 (1989) 'Of the gases that contribute to the greenhouse effect and/or acid rain, vehicle emissions account for 16 per cent of the total UK production of carbon dioxide, 45 per cent of nitrogen oxides, 28 per cent of hydrocarbons, and 85 per cent of carbon monoxide.' Small countryside roads are not designed to take large volumes of private cars, therefore congestion is common. In slow-moving or congested traffic, pollution levels are greater. Traffic jams are visually polluting, intruding on scenic beauty. The increased volume of private motor cars in rural areas can create intolerable noise levels, disruption of daily life to the local community and endanger lives. The private motor car also brings with it a number of by-products. For example, car parks, lay-bys, signposts and garages, can all add to visual pollution in the countryside.

In Figure 3.4 Beioley and Denman (1995) have identified the four main aims of sustainable traffic and transportation management.

It is unrealistic to expect operators of physical settings to prohibit private cars completely, as the majority of visitors will, whatever action is taken, still arrive by private car. However, operators should carefully consider the design and size of the car parks and the existing traffic control systems to ensure that the flow of cars and parking are as unobtrusive as possible. The physical setting must be well signposted and routeing chosen carefully to prevent local congestion.

Operators can promote and support public transport and more environmentally friendly transport methods. Case Study 3.12 is an example of how car-users have been discriminated against at the Earth Centre in favour of visitors using more environmentally friendly modes of transport.

In highlighting the Tarka Project, Devon, Case Study 3.13 shows how the

After unloading luggage, cars at Center Parcs Eleveden Holiday Village must be parked at the main entrance. Bikes can be rented, making travelling within the village more enjoyable, safe and interesting for visitors

- Management of the flow of cars and parking, making both as unobtrusive as possible.
- Reduction of the proportion of visitors arriving by car, in favour of more environmentally friendly modes of transport.
- Support of local, rural transport services through the use of income generated by tourism.
- Provision of alternative means of transport to visitors and making travelling to and within the tourist area more enjoyable and interesting.

Figure 3.4   Sustainable traffic management requirements. *Source: Beioley and Denman (1995)*

CASE STUDY 3.12

Journey to the centre of the earth

The Earth Centre is a visitor centre in England that explores the possibilities for a sustainable future. It demonstrates how both today and in the future we can sustain and improve our lifestyles without destructive processes. The centre encourages its visitors to use public transport, which is seen as more sustainable than the private car, by offering reduced admission charges for those arriving by train, coach or bike. Cost of admission is as follows:

Adults	£8.95
Children	£6.95
OAPs	£4.95
Family ticket	£30.00
Adults by coach	£5.95
Children by coach	£4.95
Visitors by rail or bike	£4.95

Source: Earth Centre, Kilner's Bridge, Doncaster Road, Denaby Main, South Yorkshire, DN12 4DY

CASE STUDY 3.13

The Tarka Project

The Tarka Project was set up by Devon County Council in England. It is an integrated conservation, recreation and tourism initiative. A key aim of the Tarka Project, named after the classic story of Tarka the otter, is to persuade visitors to leave their cars at home when entering Tarka Country. The 'Tarka Line', an extension to the national railway service, which runs for 40 miles between Exeter and Barnstaple, makes it possible for visitors to arrive at the physical setting by train. To support this service, local accommodation providers collect visitors from the various local train stations situated along the Tarka Line.

To encourage travel on foot the project has produced a 'Tarka Trail: Walkers' Guide'. This guide includes detailed maps of recommended walks and vivid route descriptions. The guide also promotes public transport by providing details of the nearest bus routes for each listed walk.

To complement walking, cycling has been promoted. There are eight bicycle hire points within the region that all provide information on the most suitable routes for cycling. An innovative two-year pilot scheme for a bike-bus has been set up. The scheme uses a bus specifically designed to carry up to six bikes and their owners. It is hoped that the scheme will prove popular with those cyclists who wish to explore greater distances.

Source: Tarka Project Office, Devon County Council

provision of alternative means of transport to visitors can discourage the use of private cars for travelling to and within the physical setting.

Purchasing power

Purchasing policies can make an important contribution to environmental management. With careful consideration of how buying power is used, it is possible to make savings, support the local community and reduce waste. This can be achieved by building a relationship with suppliers to ensure that products are of suitable environmental quality and yet still perform their purpose.

An operator should not try to change all purchase areas at once but should tackle them in a systematic way. Williams and Shaw (1996) recommends that each product or service be put through the same process which entails:

- Understanding what you need to buy and the environmental impacts associated with the product.
- Researching alternatives.
- Obtaining samples of products and testing them to decide if they perform as well as the original products or services.
- Informing the supplier of the operator's environmental purchasing policy. Ask if they can supply a suitable alternative at a similar price.

- Avoid products made with, or containing, environmentally damaging materials.
- Buy energy-efficient equipment.
- Buy only what is needed.
- Buy material of an appropriate quality to reduce defective material.
- Buy locally where possible to support the local community and to reduce transportation.
- Buy in appropriate quantities – too small quantities will increase transport costs, too large may result in spoilage.
- Buy for energy efficiency.
- Buy recycled products or products in recycled packaging where at all possible.
- Buy products which are made from and packaged in materials that are recyclable.
- Consider renting rather than buying.
- Minimize packaging where possible.
- Avoid disposable products.

Figure 3.5 Purchasing principles. *Source: Kirk (1996)*

Figure 3.5 lists environmental purchasing principles. The ultimate goal of a green purchasing policy is environmental improvement, and in changing purchasing policies it is possible to shift suppliers' views and improve the operators' image whilst benefiting the local economy. Choosing local suppliers over national suppliers may not always be the most cost-effective. However, in using local suppliers personal relationships are formed to allow a better service, transportation distances of supplies are cut and the local economy is supported. Supporting local craftsmen and selling local produce can also help sustain the local economy. In supporting the local economy, the local environment benefits since a healthy economy can sustain a well-cared-for environment.

Paper is a product that all operators will need to purchase, and recycled paper is not always an option. The Top Tree Initiative highlighted in Case Study 3.14 offers operators an alternative environmentally-friendly option.

If food is prepared for visitors, operators should try to use local produce as much as possible. Through promoting the local food, not only are local agricultural practices supported, but local traditions too.

Summary

The ever-increasing demands for recreation activities in the countryside have caused widespread negative environmental impacts but also have the potential to create positive environmental impacts. Whilst theories of sustainable development have developed apace, practical efforts have lagged behind. This chapter has shown how practical measures at a local level can contribute to sustainable tourism in the countryside. If a symbiotic relationship between tourism and the countryside is to be created, management actions used to reduce problems and promote benefits must be sought.

Visitor management, mindful of the capacity of the physical setting, is an

CASE STUDY 3.14

Toptree initiative

A Toptree token

The Toptree Initiative aims to offer environmentally friendly paper products, helping businesses to restore Britain's broadleaf woodland and enhance the environment.

In recent years, environmentally conscious businesses have reduced the levels of tree felling around the world by reducing their consumption of wood pulp and by using methods such as recycling. Unfortunately some companies have found that recycled paper is not suitable for all applications simply because the recycling process reduces the strength of the paper. Even today less than 3 per cent of business forms are printed on recycled material. The Toptree Initiative offers an alternative way of supporting the environment by planting trees.

When businesses buy stationery, forms, business cheques and other documents linked to Toptree, they will be able to collect tokens within the boxes of those products. For every 100 tokens returned, Toptree pay the Woodland Trust to plant a tree. The figure of 100 tokens has been carefully chosen to ensure that the number of trees planted exceeds the volume of wood used to make the paper in the first place.

Businesses that return 100 tokens to Toptree can choose where the tree should be planted. They can choose the Toptree Wood in the National Forest in South Derbyshire, or any of the nine Toptree groves in key Woodland Trust sites around the country. Once they have chosen where to have their trees planted, they receive a certificate and information on the location and history of the site of their choice. When fewer than 100 tokens are returned, these are grouped into hundreds and the Trust plants a tree in the Toptree grove where the need is greatest.

Source: The Toptree Initiative, PO Box 933, Bristol BS99. Web: www.toptree.com

Produce in the form of salmon from a local fish farm is staked to planks of wood and grilled over a fireplace situated at a forest shelter in North Karelia, Finland

important tool. The soft approach of influencing visitor behaviour can substantially curtail the negative environmental impacts. The medium approach of redistributing use can lessen negative environmental impacts in over-used or vulnerable areas and reduce visitor conflicts. Visitor rationing can be used when capacity has been reached (Jim, 1989).

Management actions must also address visitor amenities. Reducing waste and conserving energy and water are important targets here. Additionally actions should address impacts that occur as a result of either visitors travelling to the physical setting or through the operations of the physical setting.

The nature of negative environmental impacts means that the majority of management actions are reactive in that only after the impact has occurred is action taken. To maximize positive environmental impacts, proactive actions are required. In using the concept of sustainable tourism to inform management aims, proactive management actions to create a symbiotic relationship between the resource (the countryside) and the product (tourism) are encouraged.

PART 2

ENVIRONMENTAL MANAGEMENT SYSTEMS

Chapter 4

An Environmental Management Systems Approach

Objectives

The objectives of this chapter are:

- To introduce and explain the concept, development and elements of an Environmental Management System (EMS).
- To describe the main EMS standards, their criteria and benefits to an organization.
- To introduce and explain the EMS for countryside tourism and recreation developed in Chapters 6 to 10.
- To explain how the EMS can be used and to describe the resources required to develop it.

This chapter describes how and why environmental management systems are developed and provides the basis for the detailed chapters on the different elements of an EMS.

Introduction

Countryside sites are managed in many different ways and for many different reasons. The main objectives may be commercial-, conservation- or recreation-oriented; more commonly there is a mix of all three aspects. Each objective requires different management techniques, resources and planning considerations. The environmental issues arising from these aspects of countryside use, in particular recreation, have been addressed in previous chapters. The wider concepts were analysed in Chapter 2 and the issues at the site level were discussed in Chapter 3. In this chapter the concept of an environmental management system is introduced. The key point of an EMS is that it provides a systematic approach by which the wider environmental issues and specific local responses can be incorporated into the long-term strategies and day-to-day operations of countryside tourism and recreation sites.

Issues of sustainability and protection of the natural environment are becoming more important considerations for many industries, especially those that may impact directly on the countryside. There is now also the added pressure on managers, from many directions, to do something immediately to reduce their environmental impacts, as well as to contribute to profit or other organizational aims. However, this often consists of many isolated activities which have no unifying direction. The formulation of policies and clear priorities and the ability to justify them is the most important step of environmental management, but this step is often neglected.

Management and environmental management systems

Environmental management is a concept that has been around since the 1970s. Its development has been assisted by the introduction of environmental legislation and the need for organizations to avoid prosecution for contravention of the legislation. Pressure to improve environmental performance is now increasingly from employees, the public, customers, the government and a range of international groups. Environmental compliance audits were one of the first management developments; these were primarily aimed at assessing a company's compliance with legislation. As the environment has become a bigger issue for industry, a more holistic approach has been developed in the form of the EMS.

The important characteristic of a system is that it connects its constituent parts in a logical and methodical sequence, in contrast to casual or sporadic methods of management. A management system is a method of structuring and processing the planning and day-to-day practices of a company or a section within a company. An EMS specifically aims to identify and incorporate the management of environmental issues and consequences related to an organization's operations within its management framework. The key is to integrate environmental management within the whole management framework.

Environmental management systems have been developed and implemented to ensure that risks to the environment posed by specific organizations are identified and minimized. An EMS is a tool which a company can use to ensure it is complying with environmental legislation and minimizing its impact on the environment. They are particularly relevant for organizations which are keen on making a serious effort towards improvement of environmental performance and becoming involved in environmental matters. This commitment can be demonstrated externally by a company having their system certified by a third party.

EMS requirements are based on the management philosophy known as the Deming Cycle. This consists of four points of simple and sound management practice summarized as: Plan–Do–Check–Act. These points, illustrated in Figure 4.1, are common sense, but are often not adhered to.

The whole EMS is based around the environmental policy of an organization. This identifies and states the environmental commitments the organization intends taking. The policy then provides the direction for the remaining Plan–Do–Check–Act elements of an EMS which creates a closed-loop system of

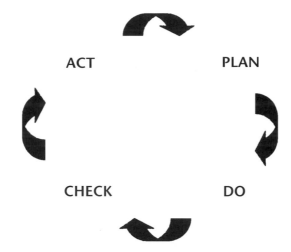

ACT   PLAN

CHECK   DO

Figure 4.1   The Deming Cycle

management. The 'Plan' is an assessment of the environmental impact of the organization leading to a plan of environmental performance improvements. 'Doing' ensures that the actions identified in the plan are carried out. The 'Check' defines the checking and corrective action part of the system which is simply an audit of the previous sections of the Deming Cycle. An EMS requires verification or assessment of some kind: this should be carried out internally through the audit and review process. The audit will assess how successfully the commitments and direction set out in the organization's environmental policy are being followed and developed. 'Acting' is where the conclusions of the check are reviewed and acted upon. The review establishes what should be changed to improve the EMS and how the process should move forward. This final stage is the implementation of corrective action and subsequent monitoring which forms the closed loop system of management. This leads back into a new planning session, creating a cycle of management practice. An EMS however, is simply a management framework and as such will not deliver specific improvement: this is achieved through introducing objectives and actions into this cycle.

There is also the option of obtaining external verification or certification; this is required for a company or site to be certified to a specific standard such as ISO14001 or EMAS. This gives the applicant the opportunity to demonstrate their environmental performance to a wider audience. The criteria for an EMS is essentially 'Say what you do, do what you say and prove that you do it' (ILAM, 1998). Verification, whether internal or external, is the way of proving that environmental management is being carried out.

Development of Environmental Management Systems

The British Standard 'BS 7750: 1994, Specifications for environmental management systems' was the first environmental management standard against which a certificate could be awarded. This drew upon the quality management system BS 5750 standard which is now entitled BS EN ISO 9000. BS 7750 was designed for application to the manufacturing industry but was written in a generic way as to be applicable to most types of organization.

In 1996 the International Standards Organisation published 'ISO 14001:1996, Environmental management systems, specification with guidance for use' as the international standard. The European standardization body, the Committee for European Normalisation (CEN) accepted ISO 14001 as its EMS standard in 1997, and consequently BS 7750 has been withdrawn. This standard is designed for all types and sizes of organization, and to accommodate diverse geographical, cultural and social conditions, it is not restricted to one site but covers the whole organization. It is intended that implementation will result in continual improvement of environmental performance, in balance with socio-economic needs. Figure 4.2 illustrates the standard's structure.

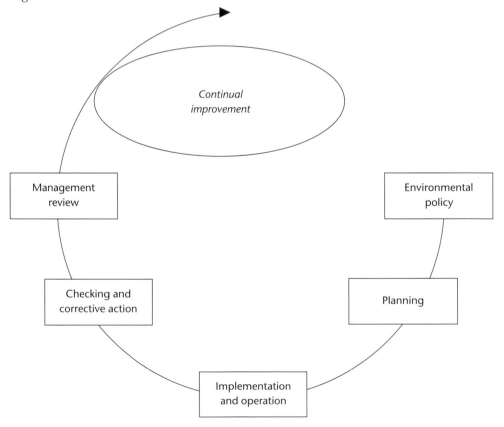

Figure 4.2　System model for ISO 14001 standard. *Source: adapted from BSI (1996)*

The criteria of the standard include the following key points:

- establishing an environmental policy;
- identifying the environmental aspects arising from the organization's past and current activities and determining the environmental significance of aspects;
- establishing a structure and programme to implement the policy and achieve objectives and targets;
- ensuring the EMS remains appropriate, through undertaking an audit and review and instigating corrective action (BSI, 1996).

A successful implementation of these criteria results in the organization being granted certification to the ISO 14001 standard by an environmental verifier. This cannot be attached to any products of the company however.

Parallel to this initiative, the Eco-Management and Audit Scheme (EMAS) was introduced and launched by the European Commission in 1993. For EMAS each site of an organization must be separately accredited. It is also only currently available for a few specific industries such as mining and quarrying, manufacturing industry, power supply, and waste treatment. In the UK it is now also available for local authorities, but is not available for service industries such as tourism or recreation.

To encourage managers to develop good practice and improve environmental performance, four areas of potential improvement are highlighted by EMAS. These are: product design, manufacturing processes, energy and raw materials, and direct environmental effects (DoE, 1997a). The EMS is achieved through a seven-stage process which is similar to that expected for the international standard. The constituent parts of EMAS are environmental policy; review; programme; management system; audit; and the environmental statement. These are illustrated in Figure 4.3. These first six stages must be completed before the seventh stage, validation, can take place.

Validation is obtained through an accredited verifier evaluating the site's environmental statement. A report is submitted to the Competent Body, the overseeing organization within each country, which checks compliance with the environment enforcement authorities before giving the organization permission to use a Statement of Participation.

The concept of using an EMS standard for tourism awards is very appropriate, since this method ensures companies have to manage their own environmental agenda and commitments, rather than simply aiming to comply with external pressures. Recent proposals have investigated an EMS award for ski areas (Todd and Williams, 1996) and for recreation in forests (Tribe, 1998). The World Travel and Tourism Council is developing the Green Globe award for the overall tourism industry (Green Globe, 1999) although this is currently being developed mainly in the hotel sector. Case Study 4.1 demonstrates how Center Parcs has incorporated an EMS into their management framework.

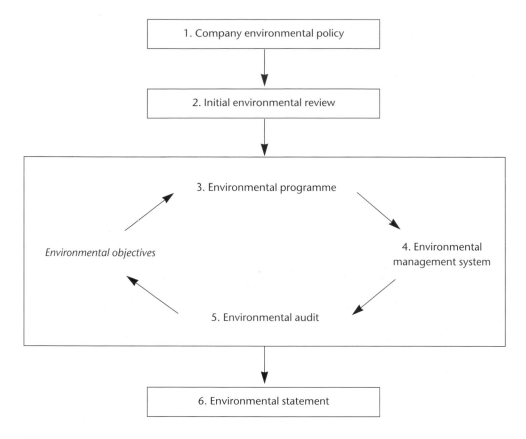

Figure 4.3 System diagram for EMAS. *Source: adapted from Department of the Environment (1996b)*

Benefits of an EMS for an organization

Incorporating an EMS into the management structure can have a number of benefits for an organization and the long-term running of a site. These include:

- Financial benefits.
- Compliance with environmental legislation.
- Self-management of environmental performance.
- Marketing advantages.
- Improved stakeholder relationships.
- Improved documentation.

Financial benefits to companies have included cost savings, particularly in the
areas of waste disposal and energy use. The cycle of planning and reviewing can
produce a more efficient and economical system for maintaining and improving a
company's facilities over the long term. Other potential financial changes include
reduced insurance costs due to improved risk management or the possibility of
further grant acquisition.

CASE STUDY 4.1

An EMS in practice

The Center Parcs' environment at Elveden Forest, England

Center Parcs, a forest holiday centre company which specializes in providing a nature-based experience, has been operating an environmental management system for their landscape management for eleven years. Below are some aspects of Center Parcs' EMS for landscape management. This case focuses on their annual ecological monitoring. Center Parcs' policy commitments include: to conserve and enhance biodiversity within the villages, and to make a positive contribution to the global environment by efforts at a local level.

Plan

The aim is to develop a natural area the company can be proud of. The ecological monitoring system starts with a baseline assessment of any valuable habitat fragments or wildlife present at a resort village before construction. Also a structured prioritization of actions utilizes limited manpower to ensure the highest and most efficient ecological return.

Do

The management programme contains detailed biodiversity actions developed with reference to the UK Biodiversity Action Plan. Center Parcs operates a Biodiversity Sensitive Area (BSA) protocol, which is in place to ensure protection of nationally important or legally protected species. No-go areas are created to implement BSA and are clearly identified to ground staff through large-scale colour plans. Ground staff are trained annually in BSA management.

Check

Center Parcs forest villages are regularly monitored by the ecology manager and external environmental consultants who assist in the formulation of management recommendations. The whole system is reviewed quarterly by all the key players in the organization. This involves the estate manager, landscape architect, ecologist and the accountants.

Act

The results of the monitoring and recommendations become a principal part of the Grounds Manager's annual work plan.

The EMS developed by Center Parcs for their landscape management has proved successful because recommendations form the basis for annual work plans. Involvement of all the key players ensures equal importance is given to the robber fly as to the forestry thinning programme.

Source: Collins (2000)

Compliance with environmental legislation is one of the main incentives for organizations to improve environmental performance. An EMS will assist in identifying and meeting legislative requirements, avoidance of accidents and consequential fines, and in anticipating future legislation.

Self-management of environmental performance through an EMS can ensure a company is more proactive towards environmental problems and issues. It is preferable for an organization to instigate changes rather than reacting to external pressures to influence policy direction.

Marketing advantages can be gained through enhanced environmental management. An EMS can offer a public demonstration of a commitment to protecting the environment and to sustainability. Private companies can gain marketing advantages over competitors and better public relations through demonstrating to customers that their environmental demands are being met. The popularity of EMS standards such as ISO 14001 is increasing and in some industries it is becoming a benchmark of management excellence in a similar way as BS EN ISO 9000 is for quality assurance.

Improved stakeholder relationships can be gained though working with customers, the general public, user groups, suppliers, employees and regulatory bodies: this can help to achieve consensus on issues and projects, and it can result in valuable input from a range of stakeholders and reduce conflicts. Employees can also gain satisfaction from working for an organization which aims to reduce environmental impacts and encourages suggestions and input from all levels of staff. There may also be greater job security if costs have been cut.

Documentation is often required for a variety of reasons such as grant applications and environmental impact assessments. The reporting system required for the EMS will mean that much of this information will be easily to hand. An EMS can provide a framework for collating and using information which has been recorded for previous projects.

An environmental management system for countryside tourism and recreation

The key aim of the EMS guidelines contained in Chapters 6 to 10 is to manage the environmental consequences of countryside tourism and recreation at a specific site. The guidelines are structured in accordance with the four points of the

Deming Cycle and have been tailored specifically for and in consultation with the countryside tourism sector.

The actions, procedures and targets developed within an EMS cycle will be unique to different industries, locations and individual sites. EMAS and ISO 14001 standards were originally developed for heavy industry and the manufacturing sector and do not therefore provide adequate assistance to the service sector, or to management directly involved in the countryside. The structure of the EMS guidance notes in this book are therefore designed to fill this gap and focus specifically on environmental management of countryside tourism and recreation.

Developing and using the environmental management system for countryside tourism and recreation

An EMS is not an alternative to initiatives mentioned in previous chapters such as sustainability criteria or Local Agenda 21 but can act as the framework for management practices which encompass them. Specific improvements are achieved by introducing aims and objectives into the EMS framework such as the criteria for sustainable tourism.

An EMS does not require an organization to develop new procedures or methods if there are already effective ones. Many current management activities fulfil some of the elements of an EMS, and in this case little additional work is required. Health and safety procedures and review processes may already be well developed and much of the skill and experience developed in these areas can be easily transferred. Alternatively if an organization already has a quality management system then environmental procedures may be built into this. By working with effective systems already established in a company an EMS can be a development of existing systems. General procedures may have been tried and tested, and problems will have been ironed out, so that building on existing systems will cause less conflict and duplication of effort. Figure 4.4 illustrates the linkage between an EMS and the rest of a management framework.

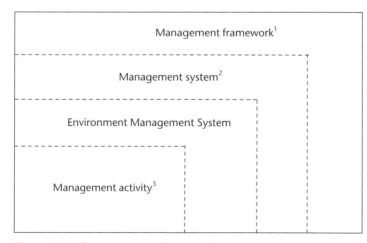

Management framework[1]

Management system[2]

Environment Management System

Management activity[3]

1 Management framework includes: the corporate strategy, resource analysis, management structures, etc.
2 Management system: may be company wide or developed into specific areas such as quality management or sustainable timber management, etc.
3 Management activities include: estate/site plans, woodland plans, visitor management plans, daily management procedures, etc.

Figure 4.4   The management framework

An EMS will fit around the current activities of management so a management unit has the flexibility and freedom to define its own boundaries. The EMS guidance notes detailed in Chapters 6 to 10 do not aim to achieve every aspect of sustainable countryside management. For example, it does not include principles of responsible forestry within its criteria, as these are addressed by many other standards such as through the Forest Stewardship Council.

The EMS and the guidance notes in Chapters 6 to 10 have been designed for use by site managers, staff and other practitioners within the sector of countryside tourism destination sites. The term 'site' is used to describe a single area of land or several areas in close proximity which have a clearly defined boundary. The site would be expected to be managed by a single unit or for there to be a consensus between a group of owners/managers to develop an EMS for a site together.

An EMS is a long-term commitment for environmental performance improvement. It will take several years to complete a full cycle from developing an environmental policy, acting upon it and reviewing the system. This will mean, however, that the process will not be an onerous task to which months of work must be dedicated: rather it is a system which can be progressed in easy stages, supporting, and not detracting from, the everyday workings of a site.

Principles

The key principle of the Environmental Management System for countryside tourism and recreation is that management will act to minimize the negative impacts and maximize the positive impacts that leisure and recreation activities have on the local and wider environment. This is achieved through focusing upon four areas:

1. *Sustainable recreation and tourism*: this encourages the management of the site to interpret the concept of sustainability. It recognizes that different priorities will exist in different areas. However, management schemes should take account of the following aspects of sustainability:
    * The visitor impact on the immediate tourism site, for example vegetation damage.
    * The off-site impacts of running the site, for example visitor transport.
    * The contribution of site activities to the sustainability of the local economy, for example providing custom for local suppliers.
2. *Multi-use*: supports responsible management of other site uses, such as forestry or agriculture.
3. *Education*: environmental education of employees and visitors.
4. *Community*: consideration of partnership arrangements to enable local communities to benefit.

Recreation facilities at a countryside site

The elements of the Environmental Management System

The elements of the system for countryside tourism and recreation have been organized to complement the EMAS and the ISO 14001 standard for application to this sector. The EMS elements are illustrated in Figure 4.5.

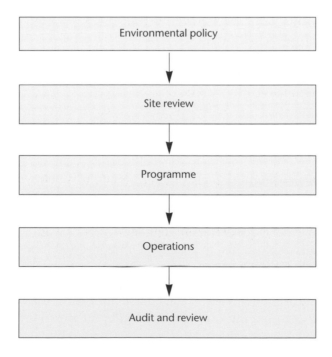

Figure 4.5   The environmental management system

The environmental policy is the first stage in developing the EMS: this is the statement of environmental commitments for the organization and the management of the site. The policy will act as a guide to help the organization develop its aims and objectives. It will describe principles and intentions and provide the direction for action. The policy should be company-wide and seen as an integral part of the organization's overall strategy. A major aim of an EMS policy is the minimizing of environmental impacts. The documented result of this part of the EMS is a written policy statement framing the environmental commitments for the management of the site. (See Chapter 6 for detailed guidelines and examples.)

The site review will provide an assessment of the current environmental status of the site and the performance of the organization's environmental management. It should identify the significant environmental impacts of running the site. All future developments and changes will be measured against the benchmarks established here. The documented result will be a report on the state of the site's environment and management issues. (See Chapter 7 for detailed guidelines and examples.)

The programme is responsible for setting a formal agenda which establishes environmental targets and actions to achieve them. These will relate to the significant environmental impacts identified during the site review. This stage of an EMS translates the policy into environmental performance targets specifically at the site level. The documented result will be a programme for environmental improvements outlining targets and actions. (See Chapter 8 for detailed guidelines and examples.)

Operations defines the development within the management structure and system to deliver the aims stated in the policy: this establishes the procedures to implement the actions and attain the targets of the programme. The documented result for this element of the EMS is a documented record of all procedures, and means of monitoring and achieving targets. (See Chapter 9 for detailed guidelines and examples.)

The EMS has a regular auditing cycle: this determines the effectiveness of the EMS and reports on how well the environmental programme has been carried out and whether targets have been met. The audit findings should be reviewed and appropriate measures taken to improve the EMS and to achieve continued environmental improvement. The documented result should be an audit report and review incorporating actions to be carried into the next cycle of the EMS. (See Chapter 10 for detailed guidelines and examples.)

The five elements illustrated in Figure 4.5 form a closed loop system of management so that the audit and review elements link back to the policy and the cycle continues. The five elements are designed to lead on from each other in a logical and practical sequence. It is sometimes argued, however, that a policy cannot be written without the knowledge gained in the initial site review. It is an individual choice as to whether a site review is required or if there is enough knowledge to design the environmental policy first. If a policy can be created first, this can provide greater support and focus to the site review.

For a site or management unit whose main occupation is recreation and tourism, the EMS described above will function as the main system for the site. For multi-use sites with significant tourism and recreation, this guidance will offer partial support for a wider EMS. The introduction of the system should not be the target itself, but rather the framework from which environmental targets are set and achieved.

Resources required

The resources required to develop the EMS for countryside tourism and recreation will vary widely between different organizations and sites. It will depend on the current management structure, the size of the organization and site, the number and experience of staff, and how much documentation required for an EMS has been already accumulated through other projects. Below are listed some of the key requirements for setting up the EMS:

- Senior management commitment.
- Co-operation of and communication with staff.
- Competence.
- Time.
- Financial resources.
- Documentation.

Senior management commitment is important for involving all departments in EMS development and is necessary for obtaining the time and budgeting required for implementation. Policy commitments need to have the input and backing of senior management to provide the drive and authority needed to take them forward.

In terms of co-operation, an EMS cannot be developed and implemented by a single person: there needs to be awareness and co-operation from all staff. Without across-the-board participation, plans are likely to remain atomized and ineffective. Communication is an important consideration here.

The number and experience of staff will have some bearing on how and when the EMS is developed. If an organization does not yet have the staff experience to carry out its plans, there are several options. First, proposals may be simplified to something that is manageable. Second, staff may be trained within existing resources. Third, external assistance may be sought for some key tasks. Using external assistance can ensure greater impartiality and increase the status of reviews and audits.

Another important consideration is time needed for staff to plan and implement the EMS. The amount of time will depend on the stage of EMS development that the management team or organization is currently at. Time will probably be the biggest single investment. There will probably also be financial resources required for developing an EMS. The amounts and categories of costs will depend on the current management framework and the extent of changes in working practices necessary. Many costs will be indirect such as time and training.

A key aspect of an EMS is the reporting and documenting of plans and progress. The amount and type of documentation will depend on the intended outcomes of the EMS. If the intention is to gain certification to a recognized standard, more documentation will be required and in greater detail than a site may require for internal and practical use. However, documentation should still be as brief as possible.

Documenting findings

For each element of the EMS there should be a documented result, as mentioned in the previous section. The quality of reporting and documenting is an important part of operationalizing an EMS. If the reporting is inadequate or inappropriate it can waste the valuable resources invested in documenting environmental performance, especially for a site review. There are three considerations for effectively reporting and documenting the findings of each element; these are audience, composition and presentation.

Audience
It is important to identify for whom a report is being written, as different audiences will require different types, amounts and presentation of information. Audiences may vary from internal management, operations staff, the general public, children and informed stakeholders. Not all of these groups will require or be allowed to see all the findings or progress that come out of an EMS process for a particular site. It is important to assess what the site wishes to convey through its reporting and what information the reader would find interesting.

Composition
For a document to be useful, its structure and composition should be clear. The composition should enable comparisons to be made. Not all information uncovered during the EMS cycle will be relevant for use in an environmental report; some information may be appropriate elsewhere in the organization, or require summarizing, or could be used at a later date. It is important to create a rational structure, and avoid using confusing terms or making the document longer than necessary. Use of a glossary is a quick and concise way of explaining terminology. Comparability is often needed for EMS data. Raw data can be meaningless without giving it context within the site and its management.

Presentation
How a report looks will influence how many people will actually read it: the more attractive it is the more people will want to use it. This is important if some of the information is to be used for public relations. Attractiveness can, however, detract from relevance and detail if an informative internal document is required. A report can contain three different types of information: text, data and graphics.

Exactly when and how to use these to best advantage will depend partly on whether findings are in the form of qualitative or quantitative data, and who is the audience.

The inclusion of technical data can be necessary, particularly within a site review of environmental performance or target monitoring. Data gives credibility to statements if used in the right context. If too much data is used it may not be read, so only the most relevant should be used in the main body of the report and the rest located in an appendix.

Graphics in the form of charts and graphs can provide useful illustrative information: this is an efficient method of highlighting key data. The simplest graphs and charts, such as plain bar and line charts, can provide clear and unambiguous displays. The more elaborate figures such as 3D charts and pictograms are more interesting and attractive for the general public and children, but are often not as statistically accurate. Maps and photos can also provide efficient and interesting ways of portraying information.

Summary and key points

An Environmental Management System aims to identify and incorporate the management of environmental issues and consequences related to an organization's operations, within its management framework. It acts as a tool an organization can use to ensure it is complying with environmental legislation and minimizing its impact on the environment.

In 1996 the International Standards Organisation published 'ISO 14001:1996, Environmental management systems, specification with guidance for use'. Parallel to this initiative the Eco-Management and Audit Scheme (EMAS) was introduced and launched by the EC in 1993.

The main benefits for a company or site developing an EMS are:

- Financial improvements.
- Compliance with environmental legislation.
- Self-management of environmental performance.
- Marketing advantages.
- Improved stakeholder relationships.
- Improved documentation.

The key principle of the environmental management system for countryside tourism and recreation is that management will act to minimize the negative impacts and maximize the positive impacts that tourism and recreation activities have on the local and wider environment. This is achieved through focusing upon four areas:

1. Sustainable tourism and recreation.
2. Multi-use.

3. Education.
4. Community.

The five elements of the EMS form a closed loop system of management, and have been organized to complement existing methods of management for application to this sector. They are:

1. Policy.
2. Site review.
3. Programme.
4. Operations.
5. Audit and review.

The five elements are designed to lead on from each other in a logical and practical sequence. An EMS does not require an organization to develop new procedures or methods if there are already effective ones. Many current management activities already fulfil some of the elements of an EMS, and in this case little additional work is required.

Chapter 5

Evaluation of the EMS Approach

Objectives

The objectives of this chapter are:

- To assess the EMS approach to promoting better environmental practice for countryside recreation and tourism destinations.
- To situate the EMS approach amongst a variety of environmental instruments.
- To classify these instruments under the headings of 'Regulations', 'Economic approaches' and 'Soft tools'.
- To establish a framework to enable a comparative evaluation of these different instruments to take place.
- To profile the strengths and weaknesses of the environmental instruments.
- To demonstrate the distinctive profile of strengths of the EMS approach and justify its place as an important addition to the repertoire of environmental policy instruments.

Introduction

The EMS approach to environmental improvement and sustainability, described in Chapter 4, is becoming increasingly popular, and the purpose of this chapter is to evaluate this approach in relation to tourism and recreation in the countryside. The structure of the chapter is as follows. First there is a survey and categorization of competing instruments for environmental improvement, and the EMS approach is situated amongst these. Next a framework for evaluation is constructed. This is used to compile a strengths-and-weaknesses analysis of the various instruments. Finally the EMS approach is evaluated by comparing it with competing instruments. This highlights the benefits of using an EMS but stresses the importance of the whole repertoire of available instruments. It is noted that a variety of approaches is necessary to address the full range of environmental impacts.

Environmental Management Systems and other environmental instruments

The EMS approach is one of a variety of different instruments to encourage sustainability. These are identified in Table 5.1 under the three categories of regulations, economic approaches and soft tools.

Table 5.1 Categories of environmental instruments

Regulations	Economic approaches	Soft tools
Laws and regulation Special status designation	Taxes, subsidies and grants Tradable rights and permits Deposit–refund schemes Product and service charges	Community programmes, national and local networks Tourism eco-labelling Environmental management systems Certification/award schemes Guidelines, treaties and agreements Citizenship and education

These approaches function at different operational levels. Regulation generally functions at the national and international level. The next level is the market level: here it is possible to use taxes and subsidies to influence the demand and supply of goods and services towards improved environmental ends. Eco-labelling may also be used to influence consumption and production at the market level. Awards and EMS instruments operate at the corporate level of individual business units. Finally, citizenship and education operates at the level of the individual. Each of the three categories is now examined in turn.

Regulation

Direct regulation may be divided into the two categories of laws and regulation and special status designation

Laws and regulation

Regulation using the legal system involves the setting of statutory environmental rules and standards by governments so that a breach of regulations can result in court proceedings and penalties. These regulations can be divided into preventive and operational controls. Preventive controls, such as planning permission, can reject environmentally undesirable projects at the design stage. Operational controls set limits and targets for environmental impacts of activities that have been given planning permission but may need control. The focus of regulations may be the supplier or consumer. Laws and regulations directed at the supplier include planning restrictions which limit development, and legal restrictions on tree felling. Examples of consumer actions that are constrained by laws are litter and parking. For Europe, EU directives are common to all EU member states, but it is up to member countries how these are to be put into practice. In addition there are laws that are specific to individual member states. Table 5.2 illustrates a range of legislation related to countryside tourism and recreation.

Table 5.2 Environmental laws and regulation

EU directives

Directive on the Assessment of the Effects of certain Private and Public Projects on the Environment (85/337)	• Established the need for the preparation of an environmental statement outlining the effects of a development on the environment as a mandatory component of the decision-making process for certain specified projects. Although this directive is aimed at projects such as motorways and power stations, tourism projects such as holiday villages can fall under its remit.
Directive on the Conservation of Wild Birds (79/409)	• Requires states to designate Special Protection Areas (SPAs) to ensure conservation of 175 vulnerable bird species.
Directive on the Conservation of Natural Habitats and of Wild Flora and Fauna (92/43)	• Designated Special Areas of Conservation (SACs) to ensure the conservation of vulnerable animal and plant species.
Directive on New Cars (96/0164/COD)	• Proposes new limit values for the emissions of petrol and diesel cars to come into effect for new models from the year 2000 and for all new cars from the year 2001.

National legislation

Town and Country Planning Act (1947, 1990) (UK).	• Created planning authorities that were required to draw up development plans to inform long-term planning in their areas of responsibility. Most development – mineral extraction, change in land use and buildings – is subject to planning permission from the planning authority.
The National Parks and Access to the Countryside Act (1949) (UK)	• Enabled the designation of National Parks and Areas of Outstanding Natural Beauty (AONBs) which afford protection against development.
Wildlife and Countryside Act (1981)	• Gives protection to wild birds, 40 scheduled animals and 60 scheduled wild plants.
Forestry Acts (1967, 1986) (UK)	• Requires that a felling licence is obtained from the Forestry Commission for the felling of trees over a certain size. • Includes the granting of power to the Forestry Commission to require the restocking of land with trees after unauthorized felling
Environmental Protection Act (1990) (UK)	• Part IV of this Act forbids the dropping of litter and allows for the designation of Litter Control Areas where managers of public facilities may be served with abatement notices for litter resulting from site activities.

Special status designation

Many sites have been granted special status designation as a way of promoting conservation and controlling development. These designations have varying degrees of statutory backing. For example, in the UK there are designated Sites of Special Scientific Interest (SSSIs) and Areas of Outstanding Natural Beauty (AONBs).

SSSIs are sites which are considered to be of special interest because of flora, fauna, geological or physiographical features. English Nature is responsible for notifying sites and taking steps to protect them. In particular, landowners are required to consult with English Nature on potentially damaging operations. AONBs are designated by the Countryside Commission to conserve areas of natural beauty. Legal powers for protection of these areas are granted in the National Parks and Access to the Countryside Act (1949).

Economic approaches

Economic approaches focus on manipulation of prices rather than use of regulations as a method of achieving environmental goals. The key to economic approaches is the adjustment of market prices in an attempt to reflect more fully the environmental costs and benefits of activities. The aim is to make producers and consumers adapt their behaviour in the light of these adjusted prices. In this way, pursuit of self-interest can bring environmental improvements. Instruments under this category include:

- taxes, subsidies and grants;
- tradable rights and permits;
- deposit–refund schemes;
- product and service charges.

Taxes, subsidies and grants

Typical of economic approaches are taxes which can be used to raise prices to discourage consumption of goods and services with harmful environmental impacts, and subsidies which can be used to reduce prices and encourage consumption of goods and services with beneficial environmental impacts. Taxation is also a way of promoting the 'polluter pays principle' (PPP) adopted by the Organisation for Economic Co-operation and Development (OECD) in 1972. In this case producers of goods and services who cause environmental impacts are required to pay taxes which are sufficient to cover the costs of ameliorating environmental impacts.

Taxes and subsidies can be used to encourage a switch in production or consumption from environmentally damaging to more environmentally friendly goods and services, and transport is a key focus for these instruments. Environmental analysis and actions related to tourism and recreation often concentrates on activities taking place in the destination and can overlook its use of transport. The importance of transport to countryside tourism and recreation is emphasized by the Council for National Parks (1997: 14–15), which found that 'of the 76 million visits made annually to UK National Parks, 91 per cent are made by car'. Because the environmental effects and impacts of air and car travel are considerable, there are repeated calls for taxation to make transport prices more fully reflect environmental costs. In particular there is pressure to increase taxes on car and air travel.

In relation to car travel, UK government forecasts (1997) suggest carbon dioxide emissions from the transport sector are likely to increase from about 35–36 million tonnes of carbon to 48–53 million tonnes of carbon by 2020. Under the 1992 Rio Convention, the UK is committed to stabilizing carbon dioxide emissions from all sectors at 1990 levels by 2000. It is the 'inflation plus 5 per cent per year' increase in fuel duties that is the government's principal measure for achieving this stability of emissions from the transport sector. The logic is that higher fuel prices will cause consumers to reduce consumption and stimulate manufacturers into research and development of more fuel-efficient engines. However, pressure groups such as Friends of the Earth (UK) are lobbying for a stronger taxation policy, proposing a far-reaching package of green taxation. This includes raising road fuel duties by 8 per cent, cutting company car perks, introducing a new tax on non-residential parking, and reforming vehicle excise duty so that polluting fuel-inefficient vehicles pay more, and cleaner, fuel-efficient vehicles pay less.

Friends of the Earth (UK) also have a campaign directed at air travel. Called 'The Right Price for Air Travel' it is pressing for air ticket prices to reflect the true environmental costs of flying. It notes that currently plane tickets and kerosene are free of VAT. In addition there are no excise duties on kerosene nor any environmental taxes on air travel. However, against this it is noted that air travel is responsible for significant noise pollution and nitrogen oxide emissions. It is forecast that half of the annual destruction of the ozone layer will be caused by air traffic in 2015 (De Clerck and Klingers, 1997: 4–5)

Control of emissions and production of waste may also be achieved using taxation. For example, taxes on non-returnable beverage containers (as in Finland) can encourage the use of returnable containers and therefore reduce the amount of containers left as litter. The Landfill Tax (UK, 1996) aims to encourage waste producers to produce less waste, recover more value from waste and to seek more environmentally friendly methods of waste disposal.

Grants are offered at both national and EU levels, generally to provide support for actions and projects that would not be undertaken in the commercial market; these tend to be one-off activities. Subsidies (for example to public transport) are often used to encourage the supply of goods and services which have positive environmental impacts.

Tradable rights and permits

Tradable rights and permits are often associated with quotas that are set by governments for pollution levels. Tradability means that the overall quota can be achieved flexibly, with companies buying and selling quotas to each other. They have also been used in a slightly different way in New Zealand as a means of bringing economic incentives to environmental improvement. Concessions to operate in some National Parks and some conservation areas are offered on a tradable basis; this means that if concessionaires move on they may sell their permit. This gives a strong incentive to invest in environmental improvements that can be recouped in an improved selling price of a concession.

The Waitomo glow-worms cave (Plimmer, 1994: 2–3) demonstrates the use of permits applied to environmental impacts. Carbon dioxide emissions from visitor numbers were threatening the glow worms. A permit was introduced which did not stipulate visitor numbers but rather fixed a maximum quota for CO_2 levels. This left the way of achieving environmental improvement flexible, so that revenues could be protected by appropriate visitor management.

Deposit–refund schemes

These schemes provide incentives for recycling. It is possible to introduce such schemes at a local outlet to encourage the return of cans and bottles and reduce littering at a site, but because visitors often bring in products bought from elsewhere, initiatives on a national scale are likely to be more successful. For example, in Austria a refundable deposit scheme is used to encourage recycling of beverage containers. Case Study 5.1 illustrates a system that operates in Manitoba, Canada.

CASE STUDY 5.1

Deposit–refund schemes in Manitoba, Canada

Manitoba currently operates several systems to redeem some of the 470 million beverage containers sold annually in the province. A system of deposits on domestic beer and refillable soft drink bottles encourages recovery of up to 98 per cent of beer bottles but only 50 per cent of beer cans.

Deposit containers are redeemed at point of sale. An agreement in 1986 with the soft-drink industry established a voluntary 'buy-back' programme for soft-drink containers. The system has since expanded to include liquor containers, bottled water, and juice products.

Container returns as per cent of sales in Manitoba.

	1988	1990
Beer bottles	98	98
Beer cans	48	53
Aluminium cans	24	?
Plastic bottles	4	?
Liquor containers	0	8 (6 months)

? = data not yet available

Source: Manitoba Environment

Product and service charges

Charges for car parking can be used to encourage a switch towards the use of public transport. Additionally, road pricing for motorway use exists in some EU countries (e.g. in France and Spain), but not in others (e.g. in the UK and Germany). Experiments in road pricing include the Trondheim example from Norway. Here a 'toll ring' was implemented, with toll plazas collecting tolls from motorists entering the city. The aim of the project is to reduce traffic jams, noise and fumes, and improve the environment for pedestrians, cyclists and public transport users.

Soft tools

Soft tools represent another set of instruments to promote sustainability. They are voluntary by nature and attempt to change behaviour, sometimes by improved information, sometimes by advice, sometimes by persuasion, and sometimes by forming specific networks. They include the following:

- community programmes, local and national networks;
- tourism ecolabelling;
- environmental management systems;
- certification/award schemes;
- guidelines, treaties and agreements;
- citizenship and education.

Community programmes, national and local networks

The are a number of projects under this heading, many of which contribute to the positive benefits of tourism. For example the LEADER project (Liaison entre action de Dévelopement de L'Economie Rurale) is a EU initiative to assist rural communities to seek a sustainable economic future. In Ireland, over 40 per cent of the LEADER I projects were in rural tourism. Projects funded under the LEADER programme included networks for marketing attractions and accommodation, and the development of local strategic plans for tourism.

The values network (Murphey and Bendell, 1997) is another example. It provides information sharing for companies and organizations interested in voluntary standards for corporate ethical, environmental and social responsibility, and systems for their implementation, certification and promotion.

Tourism eco-labelling

The focus of this approach to sustainability is the consumer in the marketplace. The idea is to supply consumers with additional environmental information to enable them to make a more informed choice in the purchase of goods and services. Just as foods are labelled to indicate their contents, an eco-label provides information concerning key environmental data related to a good or service supplied. The rationale behind eco-labelling is, first, to give consumers additional environmental information upon which to base their comparison of goods and services before purchase. Second, an eco-label can stimulate producers to achieve environmental improvements in the products in order to gain competitive advantage. The complex nature of tourism services makes eco-labelling in this area difficult, but a number of examples exist. For example in Ireland eco-labels are being developed for tourism areas which can demonstrate that they maintain a top-class environment.

Environmental management systems

This approach, which was discussed fully in Chapter 4, puts the emphasis on developing effective management systems at the organizational level in order to improve environmental performance. Such a system may lead to certification in some cases.

Certification/award schemes

Certification schemes exist in order to authenticate and give credibility to environmental claims made by organizations and to provide marks that can be recognized by consumers and producers. The Forest Stewardship Council's trademark (Forest Stewardship Council, 1994), the Soil Association's Woodmark (Soil Association, 1994), and the Blue Flag scheme for beaches, are examples of these. Award schemes are often used as ways of rewarding and publicizing good practice. The Tourism for Tomorrow (UK) is an annual award given for contribution to sustainable tourism.

Guidelines, treaties and agreements

A variety of organizations produce guidelines and codes of conduct for good environmental practice in countryside areas. For example the World Conservation Union (IUCN, 1995) has published a guide for conservation planning in countryside areas. These are a series of guidance notes supported by illustrative case studies. Similarly the Federation of Nature and National Parks of Europe (FNNPE, 1993) produced a report *Loving Them to Death* which includes guidelines for managers for developing sustainable tourism in protected areas, along with case studies and recommendations to governments.

A number of treaties and protocols which aim to set international standards and encourage co-operation on specific environmental issues related to the countryside have been agreed and signed. Some examples of these are illustrated in Table 5.3.

Citizenship and education

The focus of this approach to sustainability is on the individual acting in the role of consumer, worker, or opinion former. Here improved environmental education is an important method so that citizens are more aware of the environmental

Table 5.3   Environmental guidelines, treaties and agreements

Instrument	Aims
Convention on the Conservation of European Wildlife and Natural Habitats (Bern Convention) (1982)	Developed by the Council of Europe (with 32 member states) it aims to conserve endangered species and their habitats.
Convention Concerning the Protection of the Alps (1991)	Aims to protect nature and landscape in the Alps.
The Helsinki Guidelines (1993)	Contains two groups of resolutions: Resolution 1: General Guidelines for the Sustainable Management of Forests in Europe. Resolution 2: General Guidelines for the Conservation of the Biodiversity of European Forests.
Convention on Biological Diversity (1993)	Signed by over 150 countries and the EU, this convention provides a framework for conserving biodiversity with a particular emphasis on protected area networks and controls on introduced species.
IUCN (The World Conservation Union) protected area categories	The IUCN has identified categories of protected areas, with a view to international collaboration and standardization for conservation. The categories are: I. Strict Nature Reserve/Wilderness Area: protected area managed mainly for science or wilderness protection. II. National Park: protected area mainly managed for ecosystem protection and recreation. III. Natural Monument: protected area managed mainly for conservation of specific natural features. IV. Habitat/Species Management Area: protected area managed mainly for conservation through management intervention. V. Protected Landscape/Seascape: protected area managed mainly for landscape/seascape conservation and recreation. VI. Managed Resource Protected Area: protected area managed mainly for the sustainable use of natural ecosystems.
The European Charter for sustainable tourism in protected areas, Parcs Naturels Regionaux de France	This charter reflects the wishes of authorities responsible for protected areas and of tourism industry representatives to support and encourage sustainable tourism development in protected areas. It involves commitment to the following: 1. Integrated approach towards tourism management. 2. Preservation of resources and reduction of waste. 3. Sharing the task of conservation and enhancement. 4. Involvement of the local community. 5. Support to the local economy.

	6. Development of appropriate and quality tourism products. 7. Education and interpretation. 8. Sensitive marketing and promotion.
Pan-European Criteria for Sustainable Forest Management (1998)	1. Maintenance and appropriate enhancement of forest resources and their contribution to global carbon cycles 2. Maintenance of forest ecosystem health and vitality 3. Maintenance and encouragement of productive functions of forests (wood and non-wood) 4. Maintenance, conservation and appropriate enhancement of biological diversity in forest ecosystems 5. Maintenance and appropriate enhancement of protective functions in forest management (notably soil and water) 6. Maintenance of other socio-economic functions and conditions

effects of actions and consequently act to change their own actions and influence others to do the same. Examples include building environmental education into the curriculum, specialist university courses, information and interpretation for visitors to tourism sites, and advertising campaigns.

Evaluation of different approaches

There are a number of ways in which environmental instruments may be evaluated. These include effectiveness, costs, comprehensiveness, acceptability, adaptability and equity. However, some of these are related to one another. For example, effectiveness and costs can be brought together under the overarching concept of efficiency. Efficiency is a measure of the ratio of outputs to inputs. In this case the outputs are the desired environmental outcomes of a measure and the inputs are the costs of the instruments. Similarly, flexibility spans comprehensiveness and adaptability. Flexibility incorporates two dimensions: at one end inflexible but comprehensive schemes exist, at the other end flexible adaptive approaches exist.

Effectiveness

Effectiveness is a measure of how well an instrument achieves its given objectives. The effectiveness of laws for example can be reduced by two factors. First, avoidance can occur. This is where the law is not broken, but ways are found around the law. Avoidance is prevalent when laws are not sufficiently tightly framed. Second, laws may be evaded. Evasion is related to attitudes towards the law, the likelihood of detection and penalties for evasion.

The limitations of the effectiveness of protection afforded by SSSIs can be seen from UK government statistics. These show that every year, over 300 SSSIs are damaged. For example, between 1991 and 1996, 2,099 instances of damage have been recorded in England and Wales alone, affecting 896, or 19 per cent of SSSIs

The effectiveness of taxes and subsidies in changing consumer and producer behaviour may depend on the level at which they are set and factors such as elasticity of demand and supply. With regard to the effectiveness of EMS instruments, the question remains as to what extent improvements in the management systems are actually translated into improvements in environmental performance.

Guidelines, treaties and agreements may be limited in their effectiveness for two reasons. First, they often fail to provide detailed advice on how their principles are to be put into practice. Second, they often lack any specific incentive to encourage adoption of their principles in the field. The Pan-European guidelines for sustainable forest management are an illustration of this. The guidelines contain six principles and are illustrated in Table 5.3. Each of these criteria is followed up by guidelines for forest management planning and guidelines for forest management practices. Criterion 6 on the maintenance of other socio-economic functions and conditions is perhaps the one most clearly related to recreation and tourism activities. Here the following guidelines suggest management practices.

> Forest management operations should take into account all socio-economic functions, especially the recreational function and aesthetic values of forests by maintaining for example varied forest structures, and by encouraging attractive trees, groves and other features such as colours, flowers and fruits. This should be done, however, in a way and to an extent that does not lead to serious negative effects on forest resources, and forest land. (Pan European Criteria, 1998).

However there is little advice on how to limit negative effects in any practical sense.

Cost

In the context of this evaluation, cost refers to the direct costs incurred by a particular instrument. For example, at first glance, laws appear to be low-cost instruments, but in reality they are associated with development and enforcement costs. The imposition of taxes incurs collection costs. Community programmes and local networks often rely on direct subsidies. Eco-labelling, EMS and certification schemes each generate inspection costs where verification of schemes is required.

Comprehensiveness

Comprehensiveness refers to the breadth of cover of a particular instrument and describes the degree to which it has permeated its target sector. Laws offer fairly comprehensive approaches to environmental improvements. For example, the UK Environmental Protection Act 1990 applies equally across sites. Laws therefore represent good instruments for ensuring widespread adherence on key issues. Similarly taxes and subsidies can be applied to ensure comprehensive coverage.

Special-status designation is in one sense comprehensive in that the rules apply equally across designated sites. However, there are only a limited number of sites which are designated as SSSIs or Nature Reserves. They therefore represent something of an elitist instrument where certain sites are creamed off for special treatment whilst the vast majority of sites remain unaffected.

Because of their voluntary nature, soft tools are unlikely to be comprehensive. So, for example, an EMS will only affect practice in sites where it has been adopted. Education is potentially the most comprehensive of the soft tools, particularly where environmental education is incorporated into national curricula, or is backed by national advertising campaigns.

Adaptability

This refers to how well an instrument is able to adapt to the complexities of the real world. It is comprised of three elements: responsiveness, sensitivity and transferability. In terms of responsiveness, an important consideration is that environmental impacts are not static. Therefore, a responsive environmental instrument is one that is able to respond to changing circumstances. Sensitivity is a measure of how well an instrument is able to fit with the differing circumstances that are presented at different sites. Transferability refers to the ease with which an instrument may be translated across different country boundaries and different sites.

Laws and regulations tend to score low marks in terms of adaptability. They tend to be unresponsive largely because of the time needed to consult on, draft and pass new legislation. Also, by virtue of their broad approach, laws may lack sensitivity to local needs. Additionally, the problems of compatibility of legal traditions and systems make it difficult to frame laws that can operate across national boundaries. On the other hand, tradable permits can encourage achievement of overall environmental improvements whilst allowing flexibility in how the improvements are to be achieved.

With regard to the EMS approach, the policy statement is the key to adaptability. First, each participating organization is required to write its own policy: this enables the system to be sensitive to differing local needs. Additionally, since the policy has to be reviewed on a regular basis, organizations can respond to changing priorities and new developments in environmental thinking.

Acceptability

Acceptability measures how well an instrument is received by those who will be affected by it. Acceptability is an important factor in determining effectiveness, since hostility to an instrument may generate avoidance tactics, whereas empathy is more conducive to compliance. Soft tools in general, and an EMS approach in particular, score highly on acceptability. For an EMS, acceptability is encouraged by the fact that the agenda for environmental improvement is generated and negotiated at the local corporate level by those with the responsibility for operationalizing the agenda.

Feasibility

Feasibility refers to the ease with which an instrument can be used. Whilst direct regulation and market-based incentives are theoretically feasible, in practice they require considerable preparation, consultation and organization. Soft tools, by virtue of their more voluntary nature, are more practically feasible, particularly where the emphasis is at the local level. The exceptions to this are eco-labelling, which is much less straightforward for tourism services than for example washing machines or paints, and education which can be less easy to operationalize when it has a compulsory element.

Equity

Equity refers to the fairness of an instrument. Some instruments fall disproportionately on particular income groups. For example, taxes or visitor fees will discourage use by low-income groups if they are set above a certain level. In this case environmental impacts may be reduced by rationing but at the expense of excluding particular socio-economic groups. On the other hand laws (for example litter laws), apply equally to all income groups.

The strengths and weaknesses of the various instruments are summarized in Table 5.4

Table 5.4   Strength and weaknesses of environmental instruments

Approach	Strengths	Weaknesses
Laws and regulations	Enable strategic co-ordination Enforce common standards Result in high compliance High profile Comprehensive	Bureaucratic Top-down Long period for implementation/change Inflexible May encourage avoidance strategies Difficulties in reaching transnational agreements Enforcement costs
Special-status designation	Enables resources to be focused Protects key sites	Ignores non-designated sites Can be elitist
Taxes subsidies, and grants	Tax receipts may be used to further environmental objectives Result in high compliance Allow producer flexibility in reducing environmental effects Strengthen incentives	May encourage avoidance strategies Difficulties in setting optimum tax level Collection costs Taxes may be inflationary Taxes may reduce international competitiveness May be regressive in their effects Subsidies and grants have to be financed

Approach	Strengths	Weaknesses
Tradable rights and permits	Encourage flexible response	Complex Running costs of scheme May encourage avoidance
Deposit–refund schemes	Provide incentives for improved environmental behaviour for specific issues.	Costs
Product and service charges	Incorporates environmental costs into market prices	May encounter consumer resistance
Community programmes and local networks	Encourages sensitivity to local conditions Improve communications between agencies Encourage participation	May lack effectiveness Costs
Tourism eco-labelling	Enables consumers to incorporate environmental considerations in choices	Tourism a complex service to label Labelling costs
Environmental Management Systems	Agenda is self set – encourages ownership and reflection Encourage sensitivity to local conditions	Agenda may not be demanding enough May not be taken up Scheme costs
Award schemes	Publicity and dissemination of good practice	Standards may not be demanding enough May have limited effect on target sector
Guidelines, treaties and agreements	Encourage co-operation Provide agenda for action Encourage trans–national approaches	May be ignored
Citizenship and education	Engages with environmental issues at a general level Can encourage shift in culture	May not result in changed action

Summary and key points

There exist a number of different instruments for achieving environmental improvements for tourism and recreation in the countryside. Each has different profiles of strengths and weaknesses and therefore different applicability. This is illustrated in Table 5.5. This shows some general trade-offs between comprehensiveness and adaptability and between effectiveness and cost, as well as other tensions between comprehensiveness, feasibility, acceptability and equity.

The EMS approach has significant merits to recommend it. In particular its strengths are to be found in its adaptability and transferability across a range of situations. It is able to offer solutions which are responsive to changing circumstances and sensitive to local conditions. Additionally, its locally negotiated nature should encourage the development of environmental programmes which are acceptable to an organization's employees and wider stakeholding commu-

Table 5.5 Comparative chart of environmental instruments

Approach	Effective	Low cost	Comprehensive	Responsiveness	Sensitive	Transferable	Acceptable	Feasible	Equitable
Regulations									
Laws and regulation	✔		✔						✔
Special-status designation	✔					✔			✔
Economic									
Taxes subsidies, and grants	✔		✔						
Tradable rights and permits					✔				
Deposit–refund schemes									✔
Product and service charges	✔			✔	✔			✔	
Soft tools									
Community programmes, national and local networks		✔		✔	✔		✔	✔	✔
Tourism eco-labelling				✔	✔		✔		✔
Environmental management systems		✔		✔	✔	✔	✔	✔	✔
Award schemes		✔		✔	✔	✔	✔	✔	✔
Guidelines		✔					✔	✔	✔
Treaties and agreements			✔						✔
Citizenship and education	✔	✔		✔	✔	✔	✔	✔	✔

nity. At the same time its focus on the management systems enables a relatively low-cost route of external verification and accreditation.

However, the limitations of such an approach also need to be noted. Primarily these relate to the difficulty of a site-based EMS having influence on some of the key effects and impacts caused by tourism and recreation in the countryside. For example, one of the most important aspects of countryside tourism and recreation is use of cars to access the site. Car use has many important environmental effects. These include pollution from carbon monoxide, carbon dioxide emissions and diesel particulates, consumption of non-renewable energy resources, and the related effects of countryside erosion by road-building programmes. An EMS can influence car use. For example it can instigate a programme publicizing public transport access, integrating it with walking and cycling routes, and by provision and pricing of car parking. However, these will be of marginal importance. It is instruments such as taxation and legislation that are necessary to provide a comprehensive approach at a national and international level to deal with the environmental effects of tourism which are outside the direct influence of tourism-providing organizations.

This point may be illustrated by examining a range of examples of tourism-generated environmental problems and analysing the effectiveness of different instruments in dealing with them. A complex picture emerges. For example, the problem of litter can be tackled through almost all of the instruments. Issues such as overcrowding are locally determined and therefore local solutions will be most effective. Issues such as vehicle emissions and use of energy tend to be national and international issues, largely outside the control of local managers and thus most effectively approached by national measures. Flora and fauna may be of national significance or local significance and thus may be approached at either level. Table 5.6 matches environmental effects with suitable instruments.

Table 5.6   Means to ends

Approach	Litter	Waste	Vehicle emissions	Destruction of flora	Disturbance of fauna	Use of energy	Visual pollution	Overcrowding
Regulations								
Laws and regulation	✔	✔	✔	✔	✔	✔	✔	
Special-status designation				✔	✔		✔	✔
Economic								
Taxes subsidies, and grants	✔	✔	✔			✔		
Tradable rights and permits	✔	✔						
Deposit–refund schemes	✔							
Product and service charges			✔				✔	✔
Soft tools								
Community programmes, national and local networks	✔			✔	✔			
Tourism eco-labelling	✔			✔	✔			
Environmental management systems	✔	✔		✔	✔	✔	✔	✔
Award schemes	✔					✔	✔	
Guidelines, treaties and agreements	✔			✔	✔		✔	✔
Citizenship and education	✔		✔	✔	✔	✔		

The key finding of this chapter is that no single instrument provides a profile of ideal features. Therefore in order to achieve environmental improvements on a range of fronts, a mixed programme of environmental instruments is necessary in which an EMS plays an important part.

PART 3

AN EMS FOR COUNTRYSIDE DESTINATIONS

Chapter 6

Environmental Policy

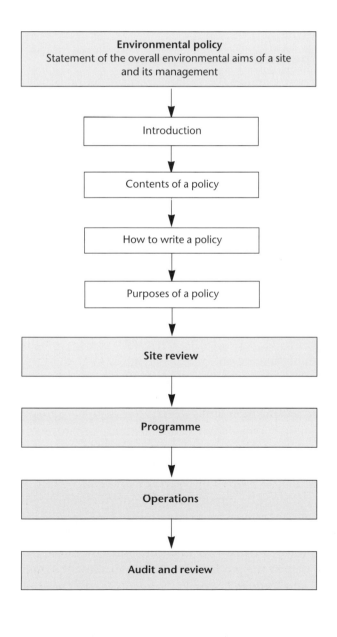

Environmental policy
Statement of the overall environmental aims of a site
and its management

Introduction

Contents of a policy

How to write a policy

Purposes of a policy

Site review

Programme

Operations

Audit and review

Introduction

The environmental policy is a statement of intent. It is a declaration of an organization's commitment to environmental protection and the improvement of the environmental performance of recreation and tourism for which it is responsible. The correct construction of a policy is important since it provides the guidance and direction for the entire Environmental Management System.

This chapter initially identifies the contents of a policy and identifies typical issues that should be included in a policy. Next it addresses the process of writing a policy, and finally it examines the purposes of a policy. Case studies are used to illustrate many of these points.

Contents of the environmental policy

A policy should be relevant to the specific environmental issues that relate to an organization's site, and the tourism and recreation activities that take place on that site.

There are some general principles that should be included in an organization's environmental policy. At the heart of a policy should be a commitment to manage tourism and recreation activities so as to minimise their negative impacts on the environment and maximize their positive impacts. A policy statement is also a good opportunity for an organization to commit itself to the inclusion of stakeholders in the process of environmental management. It additionally provides an opportunity to note formally the important role to be played by suppliers and sub-contractors in the achievement of environmental improvement. It should also be noted that there should be no significant omissions in an environmental policy. This is important because an EMS is based on a self-generated agenda of environmental management. It would therefore be possible for an organization to demonstrate a functioning environmental management system whilst avoiding some key environmental issues, by having a relatively undemanding policy. The requirement of no significant omissions is designed to prevent this.

Figure 6.1 outlines the main features that should be addressed in a policy.

Whilst the term 'policy' is the main one used by environmental management systems, there are several other terms which cover similar territory. For some organizations, expressions such as 'environmental aims', 'environmental goals', 'environmental mission' or environmental principles encompass a similar range of ideas to those contained in an environmental policy. Case Study 6.1 shows the environmental principles written by the Forest and Park Service of Finland. It can be seen that they include a commitment to continual improvement in environmental protection, and references to the provision of open information and the improvement in the knowledge and skills of both staff and contractors.

There may already exist policies and guidelines produced by other organizations which can help in the production of an environmental policy. For example, the World Travel and Tourism Council's *Agenda 21 for the Travel and Tourism Indus-*

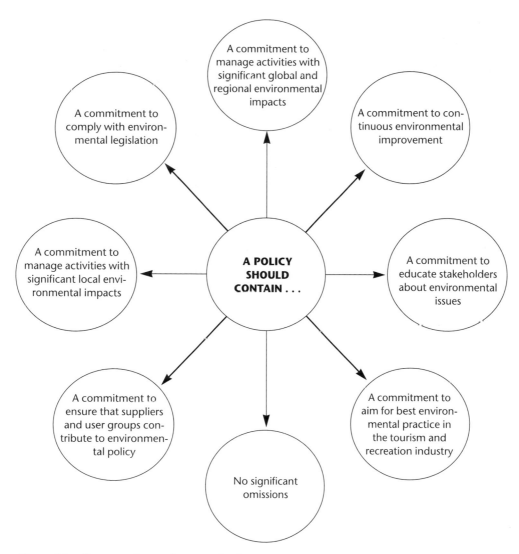

Figure 6.1 Contents of an environmental policy

try (WTTC: undated) provides useful general guidelines. There are also examples at a more specific level. For example, the National Conservation Institute (ICN) of Portugal has the responsibility for establishing an overall environmental policy that covers all protected areas within the country. For tourism and recreation sites that include protected or particularly sensitive areas, the ICN policy provides an important checklist. The ICN policy is summarized in Case Study 6.2 where it may be seen that the emphasis is on protection of natural landscapes, preservation of fauna and flora and the maintenance of ecological balances. The policy which is drafted for any particular organization is likely to draw on a range of policies from a variety of sources.

From policy to practice: a mobile visitor centre can be used to encourage stakeholder interest and provide environmental education

CASE STUDY 6.1

The environmental principles of Metsähallitus – the Forest and Park Service of Finland

Metsähallitus manages, uses and protects the land, forest and water ownership under its administrative responsibility following the principles of ecological, financial, social and cultural sustainability in the natural resources. We follow the international agreements, environmental legislation and public authority stipulations. We commit ourselves to the continual improvement of the level of environmental protection.

We provide expertise in natural resource utilization and protection. We produce and market round wood, forest tree seedlings and seed. We manage protected areas. We create facilities for recreation in nature and produce nature travel services. We act on the real-estate sales and leasing as well as extractable land resources market.

We amalgamate the various aspects by drawing up regional natural resources management and landscape ecological plans in tight co-operation with our environment. By means of co-operation we safeguard, also for our part, the conditions of the Sami culture and the natural means of livelihood.

In international projects we take care that they promote the realization of international environmental agreements in the target countries.

We regularly estimate significant environmental aspects and risks. On these grounds we define the environmental goals and targets and their monitoring methods. The most significant environmental aspects of our activities are connected with natural diversity, multiple use of forests and landscape management.

We continuously develop our ways of operation and management systems. We openly provide information on the environmental aspects of our operations and the development of the level of environmental protection and answer inquiries concerning our operations. We improve the knowledge and skills of our staff and contractors in the management of environmental affairs. The environmental system covers all of our operations.

Source: Metsähallitus – the Forest and Park Service of Finland (www.metsa.fi)

CASE STUDY 6.2

Environmental policy of National Conservation Institute (ICN)

ICN is responsible for establishing an overall environmental policy that covers all Portuguese protected areas. The principles of this institute are mainly concerned with nature conservation and the protection of natural places and landscapes, together with preservation of fauna and flora and the maintenance of ecological balances. ICN classifies areas according to their rarity, ecological, social and cultural importance and their needs to be preserved and valorized. ICN commitments are:

- Preservation of animal and vegetal species and of those natural habitats that show peculiar characteristics due to rarity and scientific value.
- Reconstitution of animal and vegetal populations and the recuperation of their natural habitats.
- Biotic, geologic and geomorphologic formations.
- Preservation of migrating fauna's habitats.
- Scientific investigation essential to human knowledge development and the study of natural values that give a better understanding of phenomena.

- Preservation of sites which present a special and relevant interest to the study of wildlife evolution.
- Preservation and valorization of landscapes that by their diversity and balance show scenic and aesthetic values that justify protection.
- Establishment of genetic reserves as a guarantee to everlasting animal and vegetable genetic potential.
- Regional sustainable development promotion through interaction valorization between environmental, natural and human components. This promotes quality of life.
- Valorization of cultural and economic traditional activities through protection and rational management of natural heritage.

These are the objectives that each protected area is committed to. However, due to site differences, each area can develop a particular environmental policy adapting these principles to their special characteristics.

Source: Instituto de Conservação da Natureza, Rua Ferreira Lapa, 38, Portugal

How to write an environmental policy

Who will write the policy?

This is an important decision. It should be written by someone who is knowledgeable in the field of environmental management, and it is important that the policy is endorsed at the highest management level. This ensures commitment to the process and a greater likelihood of resource allocation for implementing and maintaining the EMS. It is also necessary to define the responsibilities for implementing the policy, to make early arrangements for the audit of policy compliance, and arrange a date for policy review.

Length and language

The document and its purpose should be clearly thought out. A policy containing confused or unrealistic statements, which have not been considered fully, will be difficult to achieve and be of little benefit. It is important to identify who will read a site's policy and ensure it will be understandable to them. For example, employees are one of the largest and most important audiences. The policy must therefore be credible and acceptable to them. Language should be readily understandable without confusing and unnecessary technical terminology.

A policy need not be very long: one or two pages are enough to express the environmental aims of an organization. Case Study 6.3 illustrates how the environmental objectives and policy of Center Parcs are stated in a succinct and straightforward manner.

CASE STUDY 6.3

Center Parcs' Statement of Environmental Objectives and Policy

Center Parcs strongly believes that industry needs a code of practice which involves continued 'environmental stewardship'. The approach evolved by Center Parcs demonstrates an industry standard which ensures that every aspect of the environment is included in the provision of tourism and recreation facilities.

Our environmental objectives and policy are:

- To make a positive contribution to the global environment by our efforts at a local level.
- To accept responsibility for the environmental consequences of our activities and therefore to aim to minimize any adverse environmental impacts we may have.

- To conduct our activities in the spirit of being custodians of the environment within and around our villages.
- To enable our guests and employees to experience the process of environmental care at first hand, so that they too will be encouraged to make a contribution in their daily lives.
- To conserve and enhance biodiversity within our villages' environments.
- To be acknowledged as setting the standard for our industry by demonstrating that sustainable tourism is achievable and by offering to share our experience with others.

Source: Center Parcs

Stakeholder involvement

Public participation is vital in the development of an environmental policy, and stakeholder mapping and consultation are important ways in which this can be promoted. Stakeholders are all those who have an interest in the activities of an organization. They may be divided into internal and external stakeholders.

Employees represent an important group of stakeholders who are internal to the organization, and input should be sought from different staffing levels to encourage participation and ownership of the process. The views and wishes of a range of external stakeholders should also be drawn upon when writing the policy. As well as providing valuable knowledge, external stakeholder participation can build good community relations and provide a sense of ownership and commitment towards the policy. Stakeholder mapping is an exercise to record which stakeholders are relevant to a particular organization. The mapping exercise should consider the following categories:

- staff;
- shareholders;
- visitors to the site;
- suppliers;
- local recreation and tourism clubs;
- recreation and tourism governing bodies;
- voluntary groups (including conservation and heritage groups);
- the local community (including neighbours);
- private investors;
- trade associations;
- local government;
- other interested parties.

Case Study 6.4 demonstrates community partnership in action at Strathmashie Forest, Scotland. It shows how the Laggan Forest Trust has been used as the method of incorporating and presenting community interests and how relationships between the forest owners – The Forestry Commission and the Laggan Forest Trust – have been formalized in a partnership agreement. The Case Study also points to possible sources of funding to support the partnership process.

Figure 6.2 shows a model of how stakeholder involvement can be encouraged and stakeholder consultation used to inform the EMS policy. Its key stages include the mapping of stakeholders, briefings to explain the purpose of the process, meetings to develop working relationships and generate ideas, and a series of policy drafts resulting in a final agreed version. A key objective of this process is to obtain wide stakeholder ownership of, and commitment to, the final policy statement.

Case Study 6.5 illustrates community participation at the Forest of Mercia in England. The Mercia Case Study emphasizes the importance of devoting sufficient time to the process of stakeholder involvement. It also identifies some of the key stakeholders mapped by the Forest of Mercia and demonstrates how an advisory panel was established to channel stakeholder input. It shows how the Geddes approach was used, with a report being available at each stage of plan-making to enable stakeholders to be kept informed. Press releases were seen as an important way of making the consultation process as public as possible.

CASE STUDY 6.4

Involving the community: the Laggan Partnership

Community involvement in the management of Strathmashie Forest, near Laggan in Scotland, was put on a formal footing when Forestry Minister Lord Sewel presented the Forestry Commission and the Laggan Forest Trust with copies of a formal partnership agreement at a ceremony in Laggan village hall.

The formal legal agreement has grown from a pilot project set up in 1995, when the community and the Forestry Commission came together in drawing up a design plan for Strathmashie Forest. This award-winning design plan takes account of the scenic value of the landscape and the facilities for leisure the forest might offer. It also provides protection for the environment as well as setting out management plans for timber production.

A business plan also looked at further wealth generation and benefits for the local community through the potential for other projects such as tourism and the subsequent additional employment that might bring.

Welcoming this advance, Lord Sewel said:

> This agreement brings clarity to the respective roles of the Forestry Commission and – through the Laggan Forest Trust – the local community in the rural development of this area. It builds on two years of experience of working together, understanding one another's position and using the combined skills of all those involved to move forward. It secures the participation of local people in the development of their local community. It brings an opportunity for the people of Laggan to shape their future.

Funding for the partnership has come from the Forestry Commission, Strathspey and Badenoch Enterprise, The Scottish Office's Rural Challenge Fund, WWF and Europe (ERDF Objective 1 and Leader II)

Source: Forestry Commission Press Release, 11 September 1998

What if a policy already exists?

Many large organizations have mission statements that describe their main purposes. If a general multi-purpose policy or mission statement already exists, this may provide sufficient information to qualify as an environmental policy. The test here is whether it addresses the issues highlighted in the 'contents of the policy' section. If these issues are not addressed, then an environmental policy will need to be written.

Purposes of an environmental policy

Commitment and direction

The primary use of an environmental policy is to give a clear commitment to improved environmental management and a statement of the key environmental principles that an organization will adhere to. The policy is then used to guide and

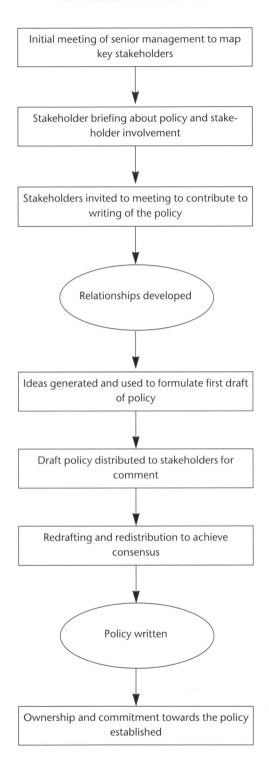

Figure 6.2 Process of stakeholder involvement in writing an environmental policy

CASE STUDY 6.5

Communities in action: the Forest of Mercia

The local partnership set up to create the Forest of Mercia placed a great deal of emphasis on involving local people in the plan-making process and therefore also rejected the idea of the top to bottom plan-making process. Adequate time was therefore set aside to ensure that local people could, if they wish, become actively involved in the process or, as in the case of the vast majority, be kept informed of progress and have a chance to comment on the work being done. To ensure that such a situation arose, it was decided that a three-stage approach would be adopted. These three stages were based on Geddes' survey analysis and prescription.

To facilitate public involvement, a wide range of interest groups and organizations was invited to participate in an advisory panel set up to guide the plan-making process. The groups attending this panel varied greatly and included representatives of the landowning and farming communities, such as the Country Landowners' Association and the National Farmers' Union (NFU) to organizations committed to support public use of the countryside, such as the Ramblers' Association and the British Horse Society. These groups had the opportunity to both participate in the plan-making process as well as the practical creation of the forest by becoming involved in tree planting and woodland management projects.

It was agreed that each stage of the plan-making process would have a report which would be considered by all interested parties prior to the next stage beginning. It was recognized that it would prove difficult to involve individual members of the community outside of these groups. The resources therefore were primarily focused on ensuring that representative groups were kept fully involved, although any member of the public wanting to participate could do so. An extensive programme of press releases and promotional events was undertaken to provide as much information to the public about the work that was being undertaken.

The plan-making process pioneered by Geddes is an incremental one, with each stage leading into the next. The benefit of this approach is that it allows genuine participation and the opportunity for decisions to be influenced by local people. It also means that everybody is aware of the issues, has the opportunity to comment on them and contribute to the prescriptions that were brought forward. By utilizing such an approach, the proposals that were eventually contained in the Forest Plan were not a surprise to anyone. They had seen the local circumstances, the issues that existed, and understood why particular proposals had been brought forward.

Source: Hunt, G. In Font and Tribe (2000)

---

inform the whole EMS. Figure 6.3 shows how later stages of an EMS – site review, programme and operations – are developed from different aspects of a policy. For example a typical statement in an environmental policy is 'a commitment to ensure that suppliers contribute to environmental improvement'. The next stage of an EMS, site review, would ascertain the current contribution of suppliers to environmental improvement. The programme developed in an EMS would follow this through by setting targets for supplier contribution. Two possible actions at the operations level might be, first, to inform suppliers of an organization's envi-

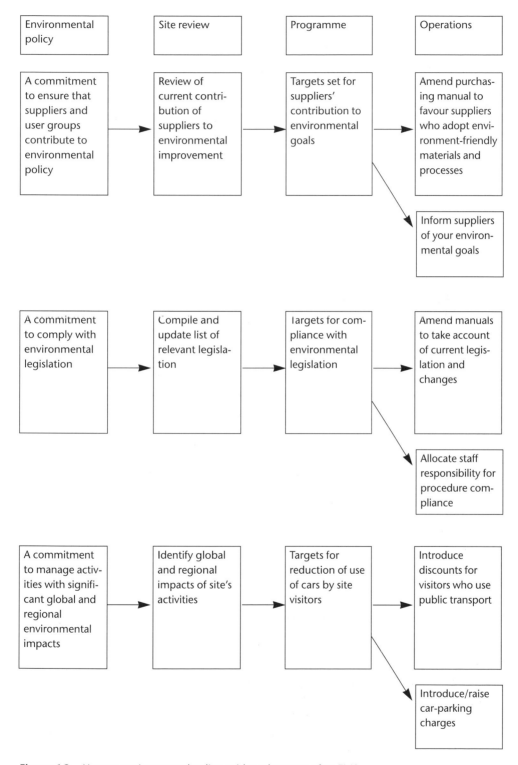

Figure 6.3 How an environmental policy guides other parts of an EMS

CASE STUDY 6.6

Selected extracts from environmental policy, programme and operations at Oasis Holiday Villages (Rank Group plc)

Environmental policy	Programmes	Operations

Programmes	Operations
. . . attention at the corporate level has been focused on the conservation of energy and water through promoting efficient use of and minimizing the volume of waste generated and promoting reuse or recycling of the remainder where economically practical.	A recycling centre has been provided at the Oasis Lakeland Forest Village for use by guests and staff

Environmental policy: The Rank Group's policy is to encourage respect for the environment through the adoption of an environmentally responsible attitude in the fulfilment of its business objectives

Programmes	Operations
The focus of future management [of Oasis] is to sustain and enhance the character of the forest, to protect and conserve existing wildlife and habitats and to provide countryside access and interpretation for visitors	Forestry practice [at Oasis] has been modified to ensure key areas retain permanent cover, and efforts are being made through planting and natural regeneration to diversify the structure of the woodland both in terms of age and species
	New landscape features have been created [at Oasis] with the introduction of the lake, ponds and streams, providing rich new habitats which will enhance the forest biodiversity and further sustain the existing wildlife

Note: Oasis Holiday Villages operate under the holiday division of The Rank Group plc, a group focusing on leisure and entertainment.

Source: adapted from The Rank Group plc, Review and Financial Statement 1997.

Programmes	Operations
A team of qualified rangers, led by an Environmental Manager, have developed an exciting and varied programme of interactive and educational activities [at Oasis]	[Activities at Oasis] range from dawn walks serenaded by the forest birds to Gaia Games where children learn about the natural world through educational games

ronmental goals; and, second, to amend purchasing procedures to favour suppliers who demonstrate sound environmental practices.

Case Study 6.6 shows the relationship between policy, programme and operations for Oasis Holiday Villages, a large-scale forest holiday resort in England. The Case Study is adapted from the annual report of its parent company – Rank plc. The inclusion of environmental issues in the annual report demonstrates their importance for the company. It can be seen from the Case Study that the succinct environmental policy provides a basis for a programme that includes energy conservation, waste management, habitat conservation and educational activities. A number of specific operations, such as the provision of a recycling centre, show how the programme is fulfilled. It should also be noted that the programme and operations that are appropriate to Oasis are not necessarily those that would be appropriate for other countryside sites.

Integration

An environmental policy can be the means by which environmental goals become incorporated into an organization's overall aims. This enables environmental considerations to be given equivalent status to other aims such as customer service or profitability. In this way environmental management becomes not a bolt-on extra but part of the natural everyday activity of an organization. In an integrated system, environmental management is accorded similar status to marketing or financial management and becomes a core activity of an organization.

Figure 6.4 shows how environmental policy is integrated into the overall policy of British Airways and how it relates to BA's overall corporate mission and other corporate goals. It can be seen that BA has eight corporate goals and that its environmental goal (to be a good neighbour) is one of these. Each of these corporate goals is developed, first into a more detailed policy and then into a strategic statement of how these goals will be achieved. In Figure 6.4, the details for BA's environmental policy have been highlighted. The BA model serves as a useful example. Its structure can be used for a variety of situations to promote the integration of environmental policy.

Dissemination

The more widely the policy is disseminated, the greater will be its effect. There are a number of possible dissemination channels; for example, staff should be supplied with a written copy of the policy. This can foster a sense of ownership and responsibility towards the policy. A policy statement can also be used to communicate an organization's environmental goals to external audiences. External communication may take place by means of:

- a press release;
- marketing materials;
- corporate literature (e.g. annual report or web pages);
- notice boards and interpretation material;
- libraries.

Mission: To be the best and most successful company in the airline business

---

Corporate goal	Policy	Strategy

| Global leader |
| Safe and secure |
| Customer driven |

Good neighbour	British Airways will seek:	British Airways will strive to achieve this by:
•To be a good neighbour, concerned for the community and the environment	• to develop awareness and understanding of the interactions between the airline's operations and the environment; • To maintain a healthy working environment for all employees; • To consider and respect the environment and to seek to protect the environment in the course of its activities.	• setting clearly defined objectives and targets addressing our environmental issues; • taking account of environmental issues in our commercial decision-making; • working constructively with organizations concerned with the environment; • promoting our environmental activities with our staff, customers and other stakeholders and letting them know of our concern for the environment; • observing rules and regulations aimed at protecting the environment; • providing support and advice to staff, suppliers and other stakeholders on environmental matters relating to our operations; • using natural resources efficiently; • monitoring, auditing and reviewing our performance.

| Good employer |
| Financially strong |
| Service and value |

Source: adapted from British Airways (1997)

Figure 6.4 British Airways: relationship between mission and environmental policy

Outcomes

The outcome of the policy-making process will be a *written environmental policy.*

Checklist

- ☐ Is there a written policy document?
- ☐ Has the policy been formulated using stakeholder involvement?
- ☐ Does the policy show commitment to continued environmental improvement?
- ☐ Is there a commitment to comply with environmental legislation?
- ☐ Is there a commitment to manage activities with significant environmental impacts?
- ☐ Is there a commitment to educate stakeholders about environmental issues?
- ☐ Is there a commitment to ensure that suppliers and user groups contribute to environmental policy?
- ☐ Is the policy written in clear and understandable language?
- ☐ Does the policy identify all significant issues?
- ☐ Has the policy been endorsed at the highest management level?
- ☐ Is the policy integrated into the organization's main mission/policy statement?
- ☐ Has the policy been disseminated to staff?
- ☐ Are staff aware of the commitments made in the environmental policy?
- ☐ Has the policy been disseminated to other stakeholders?
- ☐ Is there an agreed date for review?
- ☐ Is the purpose of having a policy understood?

Chapter 7

Site Review

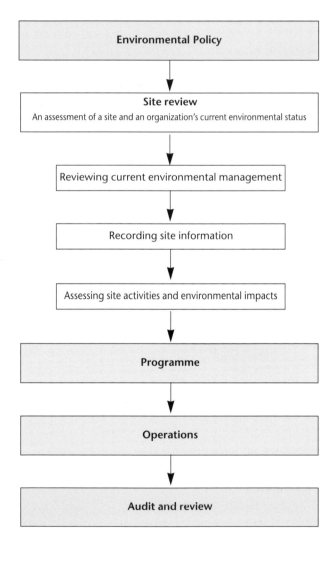

Environmental Policy

Site review
An assessment of a site and an organization's current environmental status

Reviewing current environmental management

Recording site information

Assessing site activities and environmental impacts

Programme

Operations

Audit and review

Introduction

The site review is a comprehensive analysis of the current environmental performance of a site and its management. Carrying out an initial site review is important for providing a baseline point from which future changes to management structures and the natural environment can be related to. It will also highlight the most significant environmental problems with which management should be concerned.

The key aims of a site review are therefore to record:

1. the current status of environmental management within the organization;
2. background information about the site;
3. the current level of environmental impact on the site's natural environment, from recreation and tourism.

These aims will be translated into three documented outcomes, as shown in Figure 7.1. The process of carrying out a review will also help raise environmental awareness throughout the organization. The results of the site review will be used to set the agenda for the design of a programme and necessary actions in the following stage of the EMS.

Figure 7.1 Outcomes of the site review

This section highlights factors involved in planning and carrying out a comprehensive site review. First, the management framework should be considered to see how environmental issues are currently dealt with. This needs to be established, as a programme for environmental improvement requires support by a management framework in which problems or improvements can be identified and acted upon. The second section briefly investigates the physical site, its characteristics and main attributes. Third, recreation and tourism site amenities and activities which take place on and around the site are investigated. A simple process for identifying and recording what is happening in the site, the environmental impacts of these activities, and which impacts are of most concern is provided. The impacts of most concern are significant to the successful management of the site, and will provide direction to the programme element of the EMS. The structure of the review therefore contains three separate streams: management, the site, and site activities. This structure will be carried into the programme as strengths and weaknesses of the organization's culture, framework and management processes need to be addressed and acted upon before any subsequent changes to the site can be effectively implemented and monitored.

The key questions to address in planning and implementing a site review are:

- What are you trying to achieve?
- Who is going to carry out the review and who will be responsible for it?
- What has already been done? Previously some aspects of a site and its management processes may have already been assessed and documented and can be readily included.
- What is the timetable for the review, including start and finish dates?
- What aspects of the site will be reviewed? The environmental policy statement will provide the direction for this review.
- How will the information be collated and documented?
- What are the boundaries which can indicate the depth and detail of the process?
- Who will be the audience and how should data be presented?

Case Study 7.1 is an example of an organization which has developed a format for planning their site reviews. This demonstrates that many organizations already commission site reviews. This format could be a good basis for an EMS site review, although more emphasis on the environmental impacts of a site's activities would be necessary.

Reviewing current environmental management

The first process of a review is to identify the current status of the organization's management with regard to the environment. To do this, the site review needs to identify existing procedures for environmental management. This means looking at the structure and internal workings of the organization or management unit, before assessing specific impacts caused to the natural environment by site activities. For example, questions need to be asked such as whether the organization has any formal procedures or responsibilities defined with regard to the environment, and whether there are processes for identifying and acting on environmental problems. By ensuring the management structure is able to support an environmental management system, good ideas and hard work will not be wasted.

CASE STUDY 7.1

The National Trust report criteria

The National Trust is a UK charity which owns and manages properties and estates of national importance. It has identified certain criteria which their site reviews must address to serve the number of purposes for which the reports are required. A report should:

- provide, so far as practicable, a summary of all the most important features and attributes (including uses) of the place;
- provide a fair recognition of the range of opinion about the importance of the place;

- provide a sufficient basis for all property management planning, especially objective setting;
- help members of the public or the relevant agencies who may not appreciate the range of features and attributes at a property or may not agree with subsequent management proposals;
- be succinct, clearly presented and inspiring;
- be accessible and meaningful to a non-specialist readership;
- be widely disseminated.

Source: adapted from Russell (2000)

To identify if environmental issues are included within the site's management framework, the points in Figure 7.2. should be considered.

The outcome of the review of a site's current environmental management will be a clear, focused and organized report. Not all aspects of management require assessment for an environmental management review; well-defined boundaries will prevent the production of an unusably large document and wasted resources.

Recording site information

A background report as part of a site review is useful for providing the context to a site, and summarizing the site's land use and configuration at a particular point in time. The outcome will be a report, including information about the nature of the site and its important attributes. Collating some of this information on landscape maps is quick and enables easy access and reference for future use. Examples of the information that could be included are:

- Area, occupancy, and legal background of the defined site.
- Industrial sectors, land use, existing and historical.
- Buildings, services and transportation links.
- Historical and archaeological features.
- Topography, geology and soils.

Organizational culture
- ☐ Is there an organizational culture of environmental awareness and responsibility?

Organizational structure
- ☐ Is there a senior member of staff responsible for environmental aspects of the organization and site?
- ☐ Are environmental issues considered at senior management meetings?
- ☐ Do the organizational structure and management systems enable environmental issues to be successfully managed?

Organizational systems
- ☐ Are there arrangements for assessing the environmental implications of any operational changes, before they are implemented?
- ☐ Are there arrangements for monitoring environmental changes to the site?
- ☐ Are there procedures to act on environmental shortcomings or strengths?
- ☐ Is there a procedure or are there responsibilities to monitor and maintain compliance with legislation?
- ☐ Are environmental issues considered within visitor management planning?
- ☐ Do procedures deal with emergency or abnormal situations on the site?
- ☐ Have the environmental considerations or consequences of the following components of an organization been identified and recorded?

  - Supplies and raw materials.
  - Production processes.
  - Packaging.
  - Waste production/disposal.
  - Energy and water usage.
  - Transport – employees and visitors.
  - Administration.

Job description
- ☐ Are environmental issues included in job descriptions?

Job training
- ☐ Are there procedures in place for environmental training of managers and staff?

Figure 7.2 Checklist of current environmental management

- Climate and local weather.
- Common, special and rare species and habitat types.
- Public rights of way, legal constraints.

The National Trust, a UK charity which owns and manages properties and estates of national importance, has a method of identifying the special and important qualities of a site. This highlights the features and attributes which should be considered in the individual management of each site. It includes sections on recreation use, environment, biodiversity and social and economic aspects. Case Study 7.2 shows the format of the National Trust's background report for their sites.

CASE STUDY 7.2

Summary of features and attributes for the National Trust site review

Aspect	Features
Sense of place and appreciation of environment	Whatever is distinctive and evocative about a property and its environs. Symbolic importance.
Historical or documentary	Features (artefacts and natural) which individually and collectively record the history of the place and the people who have lived and worked there.
Human health and environment	Features and activities which are critical elements of a healthy environment; including impacts on the property and those originating at the property.
Biodiversity	Habitat and species characteristic of the place and the factors which influence their survival, past biodiversity and the geological and fossil record.
Educational	Features or activities which provide educational opportunities.
Social	Features or activities which provide a service to local people; features which have special importance for local people; activities which provide opportunities for public participation.
Economic	Features or activities which generate revenues for the Trust; features or activities which generate revenues for local business, activities which reduce resource demands (energy, water, etc.) and promote local production.
Recreational	Features which provide opportunity for people to do things individually, and activities which promote fun, delight and inspiration.

Source: adapted from Russell (2000)

Assessing site activities and environmental impacts

This section focuses first on the recreation and tourism activities which take place on the site. A simple process for recording what is happening, identifying environmental impacts and how to establish and measure the impacts of most concern is illustrated. The four processes involved are demonstrated in Figure 7.3, the outcome of which is a register of significant impacts and related activities and a baseline account of these. This could be in the form of a loose-leaf manual which can be updated regularly and will include a profile of each recreation activity, their impacts, the method and result of establishing and assessing significance, and a baseline record of each impact.

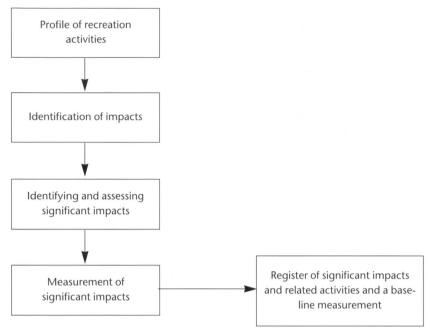

Figure 7.3   Activities and impacts

Profile of recreation activities

In this section a profile of the main recreational activities is recorded. This profile enables the important factors for the environmental management of these activities to emerge. The following list provides a general structure for background information for each recreation activity. This profile could also be tailored to review the visitor facilities and amenities in a similar way.

- Name of activity.
- Current management control.
- Estimated number of participants in each activity.
- Demographics of participants in each activity.
- Nature of participation in each activity, e.g. casual, competitive, experience levels.
- Seasonality of each activity, e.g. summer, winter, autumn, spring.
- Participation times of each activity, e.g. morning, evening, weekend, week-day.
- Preferred or required site location of each activity.
- Facilities that each activity requires.
- Participants' method of transportation to site of each activity.
- Financial return from each activity.
- Financial cost of each activity.
- Activity special events e.g. competitions, group use, conference.
- User-group contact.
- Comments on environmental issues.

Case Study 7.3 illustrates how a site review might include a profile of mushroom picking. It shows how environmental issues raised can be incorporated into an EMS by demonstrating a programme that might be developed from a site review.

CASE STUDY 7.3

Mushroom picking

Site review
Profile of recreation activities: mushroom picking

Aspect	*Description*
Current management control	None
Participation numbers	100–200 p.a., estimated
Demographics	Mainly families, some individuals
Nature of participation	Informal activity. Majority of harvests are thought to be from a few commercial pickers who sell harvests to restaurants.
Seasonality	Autumn and spring
Participation times	None specific noted
Areas of site used	Deciduous stands
Facilities required	Car park
Transportation	Probably private car
Financial returns	None
Financial costs	Currently none
Special events	–
User-group contact	Local fungi society
Comments	Depletion to natural stocks noticed through visual observation by rangers over a number of years and concern from the local fungi society, no formal monitoring has been carried out.
	It is not just the picking of mushrooms that depletes future stocks but the trampling and raking of the leaf litter that proves very damaging. It is the commercial gathering that poses the real threat to fungi populations, particularly from unqualified pickers who cannot identify the commercial species so collect every specimen and sort out the edible ones later.

Programme
1. Regulating the pickers. Either:
   - ban picking completely. Some sites in the UK have banned the activity, but this can be difficult to police;
   - license the activity. Throughout much of Europe mushroom collecting is regulated by licence. Licensing can control who uses the site, when and where, and can raise revenue for a site.
2. Protecting special areas. Fencing off damaged sites.
3. Educating the public.

Identifying the impacts of a site's activities

Once the activities of a site have been recorded, their impact on the environment requires identifying and assessing. Tourism and recreation have both positive and negative impacts on a site. There can also be off-site impacts to the wider countryside, local communities or global issues. Positive impacts will add value to the site or the surrounding area. Value could include commercial, aesthetic, natural or the potential for enjoyment. Below are some examples of positive impacts of recreation and tourism.

Local communities can benefit from facilities such as safe outdoor children's activities

Catering facilities can provide visitor enjoyment and create revenue for a site

Visitors can increase the risk of fire. However, in some sites, having more people about means fires are noticed sooner, so damage is less

New businesses can develop to support recreation needs of visitors. This bike hire is found in Swinley Forest, England

A negative impact is an outcome which lowers the value of a site or the surrounding area. These may be commercial, visual or related to the natural habitats of a site. For example, walkers and cyclists may cause impacts such as soil damage. A cafe will consume energy, contribute to pollution through litter and waste production, and may impact on the aesthetics of a landscape. These impacts are discussed more fully in Chapters 2 and 3.

Car parks consume large amounts of space, are visually intrusive and can add large numbers of vehicles and pollution to country roads

Soil and vegetation damage is a common impact from visitors

Recreation can conflict with other activities on a site

Providing for visitors can be expensive. This Portuguese vigil post for monitoring visitor safety was expensive to build and run

Recreation and tourism can lead to increases in vandalism

Figure 7.4 identifies the way in which the main recreation activities and facilities and their potential impacts can be recorded. Some of the positive and negative impacts of each activity are identified in the figure, and highlight areas that require management attention. The column headed 'conflict' should identify notable problems with activities such as other recreation forms, agriculture or timber production, etc., but not attempt to highlight every minor conflict. Revenue raised from activities such as fees or car parking charges may have a positive impact on the environment, as there are more resources to spend on the management of a site. For the same reason, activities with substantial maintenance costs may have a negative impact.

Case Study 7.4 shows how the Tapada de Mafra, a private reserve in Portugal, has identified and reviewed the impacts caused to the site from recreation activities and facilities. It shows the environmental programme that was developed and the proposed actions required to fulfil the programme.

Identifying significant impacts

It is important to identify significant impacts in an EMS since these are the ones which require priority in management. Significance is used, as all activities and amenities have some kind of impact or interaction with the environment. It is not possible or necessary to catalogue all of these, but to identify those impacts which are not only the most important with regards to protecting the environment, but can also be managed at the site level. The aim of this section is to highlight what determines significance and how it can be measured simply. This is important, as all subsequent elements of the environmental management system will be built upon these findings.

One of the initial site review tasks is to identify a site's activities and to detect the ways in which these have an impact on the environment. Completing this task should mean that the site has a record of activities and their impacts. The EMS

FACILITIES AND ACTIVITIES	IMPACT									
	Habitat change/loss	Species change/loss	Aesthetics	Physical pollution	Soil change/damage	Noise pollution	Conflicts	Energy/water usage	Local community	Revenue vs. costs
Car park	✖		✖			✖				✔
Cafe/shop			✖	✖				✖	✔	✔
Footpaths/roads	✖				✖				✔	✖
Information points/signage	✔			✔	✔	✔	✔			✖
Picnic areas	✖									✖
Permanent accommodation			✖	✖				✖		✔
Temporary accom. / camping			✖	✖	✖			✖		✔
Toilets			✖	✖	✖			✖		✖
Visitor centre			✖	✖				✖	✔	✖
Abseiling										
Angling		✖		✖			✖			✔
Archaeology	✖		✔							
Archery										✔
Ballooning										✔
Canoeing										
Caving and potholing										
Climbing										
Children's play area	✖				✖				✔	✖
Dog walking				✖			✖		✔	
Field studies	✔									
Golf	✖		✖		✖		✖		✔	✔
Hang gliding and paragliding										
Horse riding					✔					
Hunting	✔	✖				✖	✖		✖	✔
Husky sledding							✖			
Jet skiing				✖		✖				✔
Microlight										
Model aeroplanes						✖				
Motor sports				✖	✖	✖	✖		✖	✔
Mountain biking	✖				✖		✖			✖
Mushroom picking	✖	✖			✖					✔
Off-road vehicles	✖			✖	✖	✖	✖		✖	
Orienteering					✖					
Ornithology	✔	✔								
Paintball/war games				✖	✖	✖	✖			✔
Photography										
Picnicking				✖	✖					
Power boating			✖	✖		✖	✖			
Rafting										
Rowing										
Sailing and boardsailing										
Skiing	✖		✖				✖			✔
Swimming									✔	
Vehicle use				✖	✖	✖	✖	✖	✖	✖
Walking/running					✖		✖		✔	

Figure 7.4   Activities and impacts: ✔ = positive impact;   ✖ = negative impact

CASE STUDY 7.4

Impacts from hunting

Site review

The Tapada de Mafra was originally created for the Portuguese royal family. There they found ideal conditions for hunting fallow deer, boar, rabbits, hare, partridge and other birds. In recent years the number of specimens had been increasing gradually and there are now about 100 boar and 550 fallow-deer, considered the biggest herds in Portugal. Being a domain surrounded by walls, there are no natural predators to the fauna inside the Tapada to control the rising number of animals. This problem has been exacerbated by modern hunting preferences. The most appreciated kind of hunting in Tapada is trophy hunting for boar and fallow deer where the goal is to obtain specimens, mainly males, in good health. This fact is responsible for increasing the number of females and consequently the number of births. This has caused enormous problems to the vegetation, which is the deer's main food source. The natural regeneration of vegetation is now impossible, and even techniques such as use of electrified meadow fences has failed because fallow deer always find a way to pass through.

The impacts identified connected to hunting are: habitat and species change and loss, and revenue for the site.

Programme

A programme for rational management of hunting resources is now attempting to reduce the number of boar and fallow deer, according to existing vegetation resources, as well as to select the animals in best condition to establish healthy populations. The proposals for the Tapada are to encourage selective hunting. Here the boars and fallow deer not in the best condition are shot; experienced guides will give hunters this information. Another measure to reduce the number of animals is to donate healthy specimens to parks or other sites which have the capacity to receive them.

Source: The Tapada Nacional de Mafra, Portugal

should then concentrate on significant environmental impacts, focusing attention on those that matter the most. There are numerous ways of establishing if an impact is significant to the management of a site. Some of the main factors which determine significance are listed below. This list should be used as a basis for screening the impacts that have been identified previously. This process is illustrated in Figure 7.5.

Factors determining significance include the following. Is the impact:

- Subject to environmental legislation and codes of practice?
- Subject to environmental policy commitments?
- Subject to health and safety considerations?
- Affecting the financial viability of the site?
- Affecting being a 'good neighbour' to local communities?
- Of global or regional importance?

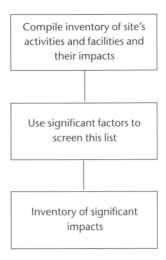

Figure 7.5 The process of identifying significant impacts

- Important? (This is measured by the frequency with which an impact occurs and the severity of the impact. The more frequent and the more severe an impact, the more important it is.)
- Capable of influence by management? (This is measured by the ability management has to exert control over the impact, in relation to how much control is already being exerted. If more control is possible then the impact is more significant. If maximum control is already being exerted then the impact is less significant.) (LGMB, 1996c)

Table 7.1 shows how the significance level of an impact can be measured. The examples use a 0–1 (No/Yes) scoring mechanism against the list of significant factors: the higher the total, the more significant the impact. The cut-off point above which impacts are significant to the management of a site and below which they are not, will be a decision for staff. This decision may depend on the number of impacts and the range of scale in the scores. The scores can be used in the following EMS section to establish a programme. Individual sites may attach different weightings to the significant factors according to local conditions.

Assessing significant impacts

After identifying the significant impacts it can be useful to record a quick assessment of probable causes. Each significant impact can be attributed to at least one activity. If the cause is not known, then the first programme action required will be to determine causes. An example of an assessment record is shown in Figure 7.6.

Table 7.1 Identifying significant impacts

| | IMPACTS | | |
SIGNIFICANT FACTORS	Example 1 *Footpath soil damage*	Example 2 *Habitat change from footpaths*	Example 3 *Pollution from anglers*
Legislation	1	0	1
Policy commitments	1	1	1
Health and safety	1	0	1
Financial viability	0	0	0
'Good neighbour'	0	0	1
Global/regional	0	0	0
Frequency	1	1	0
Severity	1	0	0
Management influence	1	1	1
Total	6	3	6

Impacts	*Details*	*Probable causes*
Footpath soil damage	Erosion on slopes and around steps. Unofficial paths.	Trampling and compaction from too many visitors overusing particular sections.
Footpath habitat change	Widening of paths. Unofficial paths into conservation area. Damage to trees along paths.	Paths are not maintained regularly. Deterioration causes users to create diversions. Lack of interpretation about conservation areas, therefore visitors may not be aware they are walking though a special area. Vandalism has risen, especially to trees, with the increase in visitors.
Pollution from anglers	Waste tackle such as lead weights and fishing line. General litter.	Lack of care and concern from some site users. Lack of warning signs promoting the issues. No policing of the area. No rubbish bins near the river.

Figure 7.6 Impact assessment record sheet

Measuring a site's significant impacts

Measurement is the means by which staff can ensure that the effects of management and operational changes are fully exploited. For a significant impact identified in the previous section to be managed successfully it needs to be measurable. A baseline measure or point of reference is needed to enable future progress of programme targets and actions to be tracked. It does not have to be a single measure but could include trends over previous years or months. The purpose of measurement is to help manage the EMS and it should not be an end in itself. Figure 7.7 highlights the process involved.

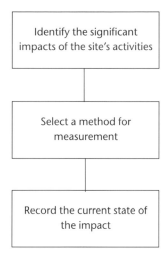

Figure 7.7 The process of measuring significant impacts

Many different measuring methods can be utilized to measure the significant impacts of a site's activities. These fall into two types: subjective and objective. Subjective methods are based on opinion and may be collected through questionnaires or from personal judgement. Objective data is either counted or physically assessed. Personal judgement or beliefs will not affect objective measurement.

Choosing an appropriate method will depend heavily on what is being measured and the results required. However, it is necessary that cost-effective methods are chosen. Resources used on measuring at this stage will mean fewer resources are available for meeting targets through programme actions. Figure 7.8 highlights this and some other considerations.

☐ Is it appropriate to the impact and the site?

☐ Is it cost-effective?

☐ Is there the equipment and experience needed?

☐ Is there the time?

☐ Can the results be interpreted effectively?

Figure 7.8 Considerations for selecting measurement methods

Methods of measuring a site's significant impacts

Methods and areas of measurement may include the selection in Figure 7.9.

- Surveys and questionnaires

- Suggestion book

- Bills and metering

- Area, volume and counts

- Visual evidence

- Physical testing

Figure 7.9 Methods of measurement

It is important to be aware of what methods of measurement and data collection are available, and a selection has been summarized in Figure 7.9. Some of these techniques may be useful during the site review to establish the current environmental state of a site. Others may not be necessary until operations are being implemented and targets met and require monitoring. Expert opinion and skills may be required for some methods of measurement, for example in identifying specific bird species. Table 7.2 illustrates measurements methods for particular impacts.

Table 7.2 Summary of impact measurements

Prioritized significant impacts	Measurement method	Site review measurement
Pollution from anglers.	Volume of waste collected from fishing area over six-week peak period. Problem area located on map.	32 sacks of litter picked up from fishing area.
Footpath soil damage.	Site survey: checklist identifying problem areas and severity, carried out by student. Key areas photographed and highlighted on map.	Four problem areas, one of which is very severe, damaged area $24m^2$. One in the conservation area, damage $12m^2$.
Habitat change along footpaths.	Site survey: identifying habitat zones, carried out by student. Key areas photographed and highlighted on map.	Two problem areas highlighted. Heathland verges invaded with bracken. Ash avenue, 20 saplings broken, eleven showed other damage.

A consideration for some measuring methods, especially questionnaires and counts, is the sample group. This should be carefully chosen to be representative of the whole population or factors being counted. If the sample group is not representative the results can be skewed and important problems may be missed.

Surveys and questionnaires

Visitor surveys such as questionnaires are one method of data collection. They can give an indication as to visitor satisfaction levels, profiles and perceptions. Armed with this knowledge it becomes possible to provide what the visitor wants and become aware of their concerns. This method can be time-consuming and expensive. However, working with students and volunteers is one way of alleviating this problem. Site surveys could use simple checklists or more complex processes using a large number of factors.

Case Study 7.5 shows how visitor surveys have helped to develop an activities programme in Montesinho Natural Park, Portugal, and underlines the important links between the parts of an EMS, in this case policy, site review and programme.

CASE STUDY 7.5

Visitor surveys in Montesinho

Policy
This includes a commitment to support the local population and their involvement with sustainable tourism.

Site review
Acting to achieve conservation and at the same time to provide a better service to visitors, the Montesinho visitors centre has created a small questionnaire about their services. This gives visitors and the local population the opportunity to make suggestions about the site, services provided and actions they consider necessary for improvements. This survey helps management staff to identify problems, prioritize and to programme future actions, including tourism activities. This process has helped to develop a working relationship between site management and local residents, and increased the understanding of each party.

One of the key features raised by respondents highlighted cycling as the best way to move through the park. This had the least perceived impact on the natural environment or conflict compared with other site uses.

Programme
Staff are encouraging visitors to use sustainable transport by providing bike hire opportunities in the locations suggested as best through the visitor survey.

Source: Instituto da Conservação da Natureza (Parque Natural de Montesinho) Portugal

Suggestion book

Providing a suggestion book for visitors is a very simple and inexpensive way of gaining an insight into visitor perceptions. This method also gives the visitor a chance to participate and highlight environmental concerns or needs. For a book to be effective, it needs to be prominent and to indicate how the suggestions are acted on. This method is especially useful when connected to a specific project to find out public perception before, and again after, a project.

Area, volume and counts

Examples of size and volume data include the amount of waste produced by a visitor amenity or the area of land damaged by fire. For this to have any meaning it needs to be compared with another variable, such as volume of waste per visitor, or area of land fire-damaged per year. The quality of raw data will depend on how it was calculated and how it is to be interpreted.

Counts can provide easy-to-interpret raw data. This can include, for example, the number of visitors on a particular day or per annum, or the number of vehicles entering the site. Counts can provide basic information for species conservation, such as the population of a particular bird. The usefulness of this data can be improved by focusing on rare or indicator species.

An electronic visitor counter

Visual evidence

Photographs can provide a clear record of parts of a site or of a specific feature. This is a simple method of recording the current state of a particular aspect and it can easily be followed up and monitored with regular photographs of the same aspect. Consideration needs to be given to weather conditions and abnormal and emergency situations.

Maps are a good method of recording the current state of the site: they can be simple and quick to produce and use. Maps are particularly effective in recording a particular feature such as routes, woodland types or planting, areas frequented by visitors, management areas, or locating problem areas such as points of erosion and habitat deterioration. Coed y Brenin, a Forestry Commission site in Wales, uses maps to record background information about the site and its characteristics. These include maps depicting forestry and agriculture, roads and paths, facilities, buildings and car parks, and constraints such as cables, pipes and drainage. The maps are printed on plastic transparencies so they can be overlaid to match different characteristics of the site.

Bills and metering

Energy and service bills such as for gas and water, are a quick method of identifying some costs and impacts; however, interpreting them properly is more difficult. Identifying the costs incurred for different units, buildings or specific tasks can give a clearer perspective as to where costs are originating and where efficiency can be improved. Service meters will provide some of this information and are very useful for a large organization. Factors which affect the fluctuations in bills and service costs include seasonality, changes to working practices, changes in the size of the organization or facilities, and abnormal or emergency situations.

Physical testing

Electronic or chemical testing can accurately measure pollution levels such as noise, effluent and emissions. This can be an expensive method and can require specialized equipment and personnel.

Case Study 7.6 identifies how different methods can be used together to measure and record a specific impact.

Outcomes

The processes and outcomes of the site review are summarized in Figure 7.10. The results of the review will be used to set the agenda for the design of a programme of actions and targets for the following stage of the EMS.

CASE STUDY 7.6

Measuring access and footpath quality

A photograph to provide a baseline measure of footpath soil damage.

Identifying significant impacts

Several significant impacts have been identified which affect access and footpath quality. These are:

- Soil damage, including erosion and compaction.
- Habitat loss and damage through informal widening of paths, creation of desire lines, and new paths made through natural areas by visitors leaving formal routes.
- High maintenance costs of paths and access points, often because problems are not caught early enough.

Methods of measuring significant impacts

Three methods of measurement for recording the current state are useful for this impact.

- Footpath checklist.
- Visual evidence.
- Visitor survey.

The list below identifies some footpath issues which may require checking in order to record the current state of footpaths. This should provide information as to the extent of the problem, and in future provide a quick method for monitoring path improvement actions.

Checklist of practical suggestions on how to survey footpaths locally

- ☐ Can you follow the paths?
- ☐ Are all footpaths signposted from surfaced roads?
- ☐ Have informal paths developed?
- ☐ Would waymarking along the route help path users?
- ☐ Broken or dangerous stiles – where are they?
- ☐ Are there any potential new routes/circular walks?
- ☐ Obstacles, fallen trees, barbed wire.
- ☐ Path surface and drainage problems.
- ☐ Safety of bridges/boardwalks.
- ☐ Improving access for wheelchairs or people with sight difficulties.

Source: The British Trust for Conservation Volunteers

Problems are identified and potential improvements listed and numbered and then highlighted on a site map. New paths and desire lines are added to the map, along with changes in trajectory of previous ones. The map could be backed up with photographs of notable locations or localized problems.

This information can be supported by a visitor survey. The survey could seek to identify who are the main path users, which user groups cause the most path deterioration, and collect visitor suggestions. This information can influence the programme design for suitable actions to alleviate problems.

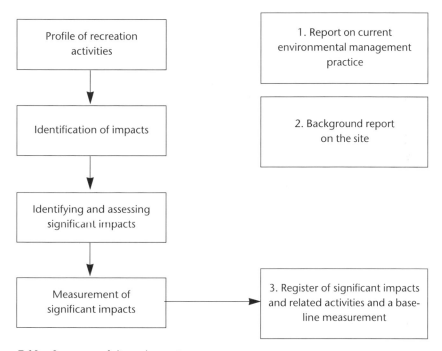

Figure 7.10   Summary of site review outcomes

Checklist

☐ Is responsibility for carrying out the review assigned?
☐ Has previous work relevant to the review been identified?
☐ Have start and finish times been selected?
☐ Is the environmental policy giving direction to the review?
☐ Has the current management framework of the site been assessed?
☐ Is there a report on current environmental management practice?
☐ Has the status of procedures for legislation been investigated?
☐ Is there a background to the site report?
☐ Is there a profile report for recreational activities?
☐ Have the environmental impacts of recreation activities to the site been identified?

☐ Has a procedure been developed for identifying which impacts are significant?
☐ Have the significant impacts for the site been identified and assessed?
☐ Can the significant impacts be measured?
☐ Have appropriate methods of measurement been identified and used?
☐ Is there a register of significant impacts and related activities and a baseline measurement?

Chapter 8

Programme

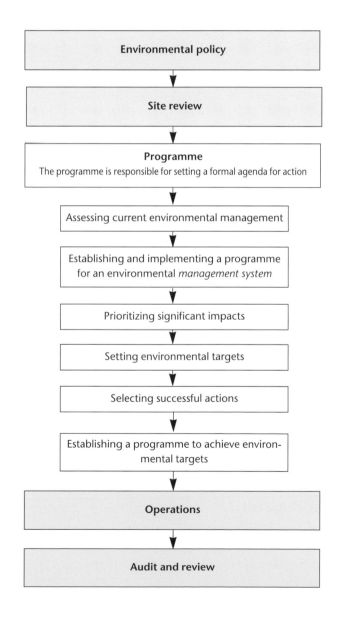

Environmental policy

Site review

Programme
The programme is responsible for setting a formal agenda for action

Assessing current environmental management

Establishing and implementing a programme for an environmental *management system*

Prioritizing significant impacts

Setting environmental targets

Selecting successful actions

Establishing a programme to achieve environmental targets

Operations

Audit and review

Introduction

The programme is responsible for setting a formal agenda for action: this it achieves by providing targets to be met and a final programme to operationalize. The programme is based on the findings of the site review. Specifically it assesses the report on current environmental management practice and uses the register of significant environmental impacts. The key aims of the programme are to:

- assess current environmental *management systems*;
- suggest methods of improving current environmental *management systems*;
- prioritize significant impacts;
- set environmental targets for each prioritized significant impact;
- ensure that chosen actions are successful.

These aims will be translated into two documented outcomes:

1. A programme to achieve a sound environmental *management system*.
2. A programme to achieve environmental targets.

Assessing current environmental management

Following the pattern set in the site review, current environmental management forms its own strand, separate from environmental impacts, and as a result requires its own programme. The current environmental management report, completed in the site review, is an account of the present state of an organization's environmental management. Specifically, it should have discussed the following aspects of an organization's management framework:

- Organizational culture.
- Organizational structure.
- Organizational systems.
- Job descriptions.
- Job training.

This section enables the report to be assessed to identify deficiencies in current environmental management. To aid this process, this section will suggest possible ways of changing the above aspects of an organization's management framework so that they address the environment.

Organizational culture

Organizational culture describes the way things are done in an organization and forms the basis for the rules of acceptable or unacceptable behaviour. An organization's culture can be managed in a variety of ways so that it supports environmental improvement. If an organization wants to have a strong environmental culture, the initial step must be to give environmental issues equal status to all other concerns within the organization. A commitment to the environment in the organization's overall policy or, even better, a separate environmental policy, as explained in Chapter 6, will act as a statement of intent and guide an organization's behaviour, beliefs, values and attitudes. An environmental policy can be a valuable method of disseminating an organization's commitment to the environment. Another method of disseminating an organization's commitment to the environment is through gaining an environmental award. To obtain an environmental award an organization needs to commit to good environmental practice. The benefits and increased awareness that an environmental award may bring with it will help environmental issues to be promoted within an organization's culture.

Burnham Beeches promotes their environmental culture by displaying the Forest Authority Centres of Excellence Award

Environmental symbols can help embed environmental issues into an organization's culture. A logo, for example, portrays an organization's identity. If in some way the logo refers to the environment, it would make a clear statement that the environment is important to the organization. Recycling points and good environmental behaviour posters and signs are all symbols that help raise the status of environmental issues within an organization. Culture is affected by behaviour, so by setting standards of acceptable environmental behaviour, an organization can change its culture. These standards may include policies about litter or wasting energy. The National Trust has been successful in changing culture at several of their properties. Litter-picks have been introduced to ensure that the properties are litter-free. In creating a litter-free environment it is less likely that litter will be dropped.

Promotion and rewards should be offered, just like they are in other fields, to those that perform well in environmental duties. This will help promote environmental management internally as a significant element of management, raising its profile and influence upon organizational culture.

Organizational structure

An organization's structure is the framework which describes how personnel are grouped together and how these groupings operate. In describing an organization's structure it is common to map it out, showing the span of control and communication lines. In small organizations there may be no formal structure: one person may be responsible for all aspects of management and therefore there is no need for a structural map. However, environmental management still needs to be part of the informal management framework. In a larger organization the formal structure can be based on the activities of an organization that have to be carried out. One of these activities should be environmental management. Figure 8.1 represents a typical functional organization chart for a forest; it clearly shows that equal status has been given to environmental management.

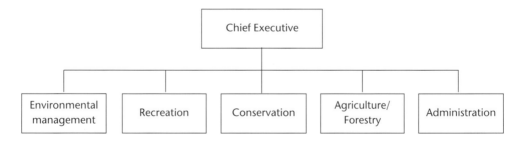

Figure 8.1　A functional organization chart for a forest

The larger the organization, the more likely that the activities will become separate departments or functional management areas, with their own managers and personnel contained within them.

Adopting a matrix structure allows an organization to move away from the segmented structure of Figure 8.1 towards an integrated structure. A matrix allows the organization's structure to be built around one or more factors. Figure 8.2 illustrates a matrix structure for a forest. Both environmental management issues and quality issues cross all departments, providing an integrated approach and underlining their significance as a management concern.

	Departments			
Factors	*Recreation*	*Conservation*	*Agriculture/ Forestry*	*Administration*
Environmental management				---------------------►
Quality				---------------------►

Figure 8.2 A matrix structure chart for a forest

This section has highlighted only two of many different management structures available to an organization. It is crucial that whichever structure is chosen, be it formal or informal, environmental management is located within it.

Organizational systems

Organizational systems need to be in place to ensure that environmental management is carried out. Central to organizational systems is documentation. Documentation ensures that records of the EMS are kept so that compliance with the requirements of the EMS can be demonstrated. Documents should form the basis of an EMS manual. The manual acts as the principal source of reference and documentation for the EMS. It should contain the core of policy, site review, programme, operations, and audit and review documents. Table 8.1 indicates the document outcomes of the EMS that should be stored in the EMS manual.

The successful implementation of an EMS relies on the transition of documentation from one element of the EMS to the next. In the first cycle of the EMS the policy will be the first piece of documentation. However, on the second cycle it will be adjusted according to the findings of the review report. The site review requires the written policy to give it direction and the programme uses the current environmental management report and register of significant impacts to set a formal agenda of action for the EMS. Operations implements the programme to achieve environmental targets, and the audit and review draws upon the majority of the documents to assess the overall performance of the EMS.

Although the key to organizational systems is documentation, documents must be used correctly. It is crucial that the right people have the right information at the right time and in the right place. Therefore the EMS manual needs to be:

* assigned to someone who is given the overall responsibility of it;
* distributed to those with EMS duties;
* clear, understandable and self-explanatory to those who need to use it;
* designed so as to record relevant data and information;
* periodically reviewed and revised according to environmental performance;

Table 8.1 Documentation held in the environmental manual

EMS element	Documented outcomes
Policy	• Written policy
Site review	• Background report on the site • Report on current environmental management practice • Register of significant environmental impacts
Programme	• Current environmental management programme • Programme to achieve environmental targets
Operations	• Evidence of scheduling, sequencing and resources allocation • Project planning forms • Written procedures • Project recording forms • Environmental performance surveys • Facility maintenance forms • Monitoring report
Audit and review	• Audit report • Review report

Possible appendices	• List of stakeholders (policy)
	• Relevant legislation and regulations (site review)
	• Health and safety information (site review)
	• Environmental consequences of the following components of an organization: (site review)
	  – Supplies and raw materials
	  – Production processes
	  – Packaging
	  – Waste Production/disposal
	  – Energy and water usage
	  – Transport – employees and visitors
	  – Administration
	• An organogram explaining roles and responsibilities (programme)

- authenticated and dated as a true record of the current state of environmental management;
- fully referenced;
- stored in an accessible place.

Note that detailed advice on writing the required documented outcomes of the EMS is provided in the individual EMS element chapters that precede and follow this chapter.

Job descriptions

Upon appointment, an employee should receive a job description. The job description should include the employee's environmental duties, tasks and responsibilities. It should also state lines of accountability and indicate the job location in the organizational structure.

It is likely that environmental duties, tasks and responsibilities will form only a part of an employee's job and therefore only a section of their job description, but all job descriptions should encompass environmental issues. For example, a senior manager may be asked to take on the responsibility of co-ordinating their organization's EMS. If this is the case, their job description may include the following:

As 'environmental champion' you will strive to ensure that the EMS is a success by:

- taking charge of co-ordinating and implementing the organization's EMS;
- taking responsibility for the co-ordination of the EMS manual;
- motivating personnel to become involved in the EMS;
- allocating human, financial and physical resources to the EMS;
- defining EMS responsibilities of personnel;
- disseminating the reasons for managing the environment and the benefits it brings;
- communicating the objectives of the EMS;
- updating staff on the progress of the EMS;
- involving the organization as a whole in local and national initiatives, attending green tourism events, subscribing to green magazines, promoting networking with other organizations that are tackling the same issues.

Job training

An organization should aim to address a range of training needs throughout the implementation of an EMS. The task here is to ascertain the knowledge of the personnel who are responsible for implementing the EMS and then compare it to the level of knowledge that is needed to implement the EMS. This will allow training to be devised that can bridge any gap between existing knowledge and required knowledge.

Environmental training, although it may be expensive, should be seen as an investment in the future performance of the EMS, and a tool that will facilitate environmental benefits that outweigh the costs. Training should ensure that personnel are aware of the principal global and local environmental issues relevant to the organization. More specifically, environmental training for an EMS can be categorised into the three areas of job-specific training, EMS training and environmental awareness

Job-specific training is mainly for staff whose work is subject to environmental regulations or related to environmental targets. Job-specific training involves learning about environmental impacts associated with particular processes (e.g. soil compaction from trampling). Purchasing staff may need to know more about the environment impacts associated with purchasing goods and materials and their alternatives.

EMS training should include an explanation of the EMS elements, their purpose, contents and construction. Staff need to be made aware of the requirements of the EMS and the importance of meeting them, the impact of individual's jobs on the environment, how to follow the procedures introduced for tasks with environmental consequences, and the consequences of not following set procedures.

Environmental awareness aims to encourage a sense of personal responsibility towards environmental protection. Awareness training shows the big picture (e.g. global warming, deforestation and ozone depletion) but it should also explain how these issues correspond with activities on the site and off-site due to the site's existence and how they relate to the environmental policy.

Establishing and implementing a programme for an environmental management system

Table 8.2 is an example of a programme to ensure that an environmental management system is in place. The programme lists the problems identified through the assessment of the current environmental management report and then states the actions that will be utilized to alleviate each problem. The actions will need to be implemented at this point.

Table 8.2 Example programme for an environmental management system

Current environmental management problem	Action/Actions
Environmental issues are not given the same status as other management concerns.	Embed environmental symbols into the organization, such as recycling points, and aim to obtain environmental awards for good practice
There is not a member of staff responsible for environmental management within the organization.	A champion needs to be chosen who will take responsibility for overseeing the implementation of the EMS, co-ordinate the EMS manual, define personnel responsibilities, and allocate human, financial and economic resources to the EMS.
Personnel are unclear what is and what is not acceptable environmental behaviour.	The environmental champion needs to set standards of responsible environmental behaviour.
Environmental training schemes are not available for either management or personnel.	The knowledge gap to implement an EMS needs to be identified and job-specific training, EMS training and environmental awareness training provided.
Staff members are not aware of their environmental responsibilities.	Job descriptions for new jobs and for all jobs that have EMS duties need to contain a list of expected tasks and responsibilities.
Environmental management cannot be found within the organization's structure.	Map out an organizational chart to show the span of control and communication lines of an organization's environmental management
Environmental management, although considered important, is not being carried out to its full potential within the organization.	Document environmental management processes to ensure that records are kept so that compliance with regulations and targets can be demonstrated. Store this documentation in an accessible EMS manual

Prioritizing significant impacts

Prioritizing significant environmental impacts is the first task in establishing a programme to alleviate such impacts. Impacts that have been identified as significant in the register of significant impacts require prioritization. The aim of prioritization is to ensure that the programme to achieve environmental targets secures the best possible environmental performance.

Prioritizing sets the agenda for the programme to achieve environmental targets by listing an organization's significant impacts in the order that they will be managed. It should be noted that prioritization is not calculated using significance only; if it were, the prioritized list of significant impacts would simply start with the most significant and finish with the least significant impact. Factors that will affect the calculation of prioritization will be individual to an organization, but are likely to include:

- ease of solution;
- likelihood of success;
- urgency;
- equipment availability;
- expertise of staff;
- visitor opinion;
- effect on the public image of the organization;
- cost–benefit analysis.

An organization may prioritize impacts that are some way down the list of significance but which can be implemented at low cost, are urgently required, which give quick and visible results, which enhance the visitor experience and that staff feel comfortable in tackling. This can help maintain momentum and enthusiasm for the EMS as a whole.

Figure 8.3 illustrates the process of prioritizing significant impacts. Impacts identified in the register of significant impacts should be duplicated in the vertical columns, and the significance score of each impact should be inserted. Each impact then needs to be assessed according to the questions posed and a score given to the answers according to the scoring scale provided. The higher the total, the greater the priority of the impact. It is recognized that a score-based system is likely to involve qualitative as well as quantitative analysis, so a space for comments can be found at the bottom of the table to allow the user to justify any decisions that have been made.

The process of prioritization can be completed by transferring the data produced in Figure 8.3 to Table 8.3 which lists the significant impacts in order of priority and asks for evidence of justification.

Your answer	No	Yes	Significant impacts				
Score	0	1	Pollution from anglers	Habitat change along footpaths	Congested local roads	Disturbance of nesting sparrowhawk	Footpath soil damage
Significance score brought forward			6	3	5	3	6
Is it easy to alleviate the impact?			1	0	0	0	0
Will alleviation of the impact show good results?			1	1	0	1	1
Is a solution required urgently?			1	1	0	0	1
Is there the necessary equipment to act against the impact?			1	1	0	0	1
Is there a member of staff that is trained to deal with the impact?			1	1	0	0	1
Will the visitor experience be enhanced if the impact is removed?			1	1	0	0	1
Will the site image be enhanced if the impact is removed?			1	1	1	1	1
Is it easy to identify the probable causes of the impact?			1	0	0	1	1
Will the benefit to the site be greater than the estimated cost of removing the impact?			1	1	0	0	1
Total			15	10	6	6	14

Comments

Figure 8.3 Prioritization of significant impacts

Table 8.3 Example list of prioritized significant impacts

Rank	Score	Prioritized significant impact	Reasons for prioritizing significant impact
1	15	Pollution from anglers	• The visitor experience is effected by visible litter • No training or expensive equipment is required to pick litter up • Removing the litter will altogether show good results and raise the profile of the site
2	14	Footpath soil damage	• Most of our visitors come to walk and therefore a solution is required urgently
3	10	Habitat change along footpaths	• The visitor experience will be improved by alleviating the impact • It is relatively easy to take action to re-route the footpath
4	6	Congested local roads	• Although the site would like to alleviate this impact, a survey showed that visitors like to travel to the site in their own cars • Cost–benefit analysis is low as income is received from car parking charges
5	6	Disturbance of nesting sparrow hawk	• Staff do not have enough knowledge to alleviate the impact • Equipment to pinch-point the nesting area is not available

Setting environmental targets

The environmental policy should have included a commitment to improvement in overall environmental performance. Setting targets is a way of judging performance. Targets should be set within the context of the aims of the policy, but also directly reflect the list of prioritized significant impacts as listed in Table 8.3.

The purpose of establishing environmental targets is to provide a clear and achievable objective against which to measure the success of the programme. The register of significant impacts provides baseline measurements for all identified significant impacts. It is these measurements which targets must aim to improve.

Environmental targets clarify the nature of the environmental improvement that is to be made and the time period involved. This means that an environmental target must state a quantifiable amount of improvement and a date by which this improvement will be met. An environmental target must be specific in that it applies to one significant impact only. The environmental target must also be able to be measured with the same technique that the impact was originally measured in the register of significant impacts. In this way targets are directly linked to measuring techniques, which allows environmental performance to be assessed during the operations element of the EMS when the significant impact is re-measured.

Environmental targets need to be realistic but challenging. There is no point in setting environmental targets that cannot be achieved, as the programme will fail and enthusiasm for the EMS will diminish. Setting environmental targets that are easy to meet is not acceptable either, as this will mean that an organization is not utilizing its resources to its best ability, which will reflect on the benefits that the site receives. For these reasons it is suggested that all environmental targets that are set be given considerable thought and agreed upon by those who set them and those who must strive to meet them.

Table 8.4 provides examples of environmental targets set for the prioritized significant impacts in Table 8.3 that conform to the SMART principles which are:

- *specific* – state clearly what they aim to do;
- *measurable* – able to be qualitatively or quantitatively assessed;
- *agreed* – with those who must attain them;
- *realistic* – challenging but not unobtainable;
- *time-constrained* – achieved in a stated time period.

Table 8.4   Environmental targets

Prioritized significant impact	Environmental target
Pollution from anglers	To reduce pollution from anglers by 50 per cent in twelve months
Footpath soil damage	To reduce footpath soil damage by 20 per cent in 24 months
Habitat change along footpaths	To reduce habitat change along footpaths by 25 per cent in twelve months
Congested local roads	In one year to identify how the site contributes to the congestion of local roads
Disturbance of nesting sparrow hawk	To eradicate disturbance in six months

Note that the site-specific environmental targets set in Table 8.4 will be reviewed in the audit checklist (Table 10.1) under the section called site-specific programme.

An important part of setting environmental targets is consultation. The same stakeholders that were associated with writing the policy should again be consulted when setting environmental targets. It is likely that some environmental targets will affect them. For example, an environmental target that states that 30 per cent of waste generated on site should be recycled annually will have implications for visitors and suppliers. Equally, an environmental target that states that footpaths will be replaced to original widths within three years will affect walkers and mountain bikers.

The Huhmari Holiday Centre in Finland provides recycling bins for their visitors. Setting an environmental target that specifies that 30 per cent of annual waste will be recycled will have implications for visitors who are expected to use the bins, and suppliers as they may be requested to provide goods that can be recycled

Selecting successful actions

The chapter has so far prioritized significant impacts and set environmental targets for each significant impact. The task now is to designate actions to each significant impact to meet the specified environmental targets in the stated period of time. Chapter 3 examines management tools in depth and provides a number of good practice case studies, which should be used to help an organization select suitable actions. Therefore this section concentrates on providing advice on making sure that actions selected fulfil their purpose.

The register of significant impacts entailed an assessment of the probable causes of the significant impacts. In examining probable causes, assessment records should identify what actually needs to be managed. For example, the soil in close proximity to an information panel situated by the side of a popular footpath has become compacted. Assessment shows that although the walkers and runners are responsible for the soil compaction, one of the probable causes of the impact is the positioning of the panel. Assessment in the majority of cases will highlight that for a management action to be successful it must address the probable causes of the impact and not only the impact itself. Drawing again on the example of soil compaction, if the impact is to be alleviated not only must the soil be loosened and oxygenated but action is required to either relocate the panel or re-route the walkers and runners.

It is suggested that before actions are selected, the following questions are asked of them to ensure their success:

Expertise:	Can the action be made operational?
Resource availability:	Are the labour, equipment and materials necessary to implement the action available?
Visitor opinion:	Have the consequences – especially user reactions and side-effects of the action – been considered?
Policy commitment:	Is the selected action in line with the commitments of the policy element of the EMS?
Justification:	Why has the action been chosen over other actions?
Compatibility:	Can more than one action be used to alleviate the impact?
Improvement:	Will the chosen action be able to meet the environmental target in the stated period?

Establishing a programme to achieve environmental targets

A programme for significant environmental impacts can now be established. The programme should contain the following information:

- prioritized significant impacts taken from Table 8.3;
- an environmental target for each significant impact from Table 8.4;
- probable causes for impact taken from the register of significant impacts;
- the actions that will be used to manage the significant impact.

Table 8.5 is an example of what a programme to achieve environmental targets ready for the operations element to implement should look like.

Outcomes

The outcomes of the programme should be:

1. A programme to achieve a sound environmental management system.
2. A programme to achieve environmental targets.

Table 8.5 Programme to achieve environmental targets

Prioritized significant impact	Environmental target	Probable causes	Action/Actions
Pollution from anglers	To reduce pollution from anglers by 50 per cent in twelve months	• No rubbish bins near the river • Lack of warning signs promoting the issues • No policing of the area • Lack of care and concern from some site users	• Provide bins • Indicate on maps where the bins can be found • Provide signs directing users to bins • Educate visitors to take their litter home • Reduce packaging on sold goods
Footpath soil damage	To reduce footpath soil damage by 20 per cent in 24 months	• Trampling and compaction from too many visitors overusing particular sections	• Re-route footpath • Pinch point unofficial footpaths • Replace topsoil
Habitat change along footpaths	To reduce habitat change along footpaths by 25 per cent in twelve months	• Vandalism has risen especially to trees with the increase in visitors • Paths are not maintained regularly. Deterioration causes users to create diversions • Lack of interpretation about conservation areas therefore visitors may not be aware they are walking through a special area	• Pinch point large and vulnerable trees • Pinch-point diversions • Introduce penalty for anyone found vandalizing trees • Introduce signposts • Introduce guided tours and self-guided tours
Congestion of local roads	To identify how the site contributes to the congestion of local roads within one year	• Not known	• Visitor survey and analysis
Disturbance of nesting sparrow hawk	To eradicate disturbance in six months	• Visitors are allowed too close to the nest • Visitors are inquisitive	• Pinch-point the nest • Provide remote view of the nest via a camera

Checklist

- ☐ Has the current environmental management report been assessed?
- ☐ Has the organization got a strong environmental culture?
- ☐ Is environmental management included in the organization's structure?
- ☐ Are there environmental management systems in place to ensure that environmental management is carried out?
- ☐ Has an environmental champion been chosen?
- ☐ Is there an environmental management manual?
- ☐ Are environmental responsibilities, tasks and duties defined in job descriptions?
- ☐ Is there environmental training available for those who require it?
- ☐ Has a programme for an environmental management system been established and implemented?
- ☐ Have significant impacts been prioritized?
- ☐ Has the prioritization process been justified?
- ☐ Have environmental targets been set?
- ☐ Have questions been asked to ensure that the actions selected are successful?
- ☐ Has a programme to meet environmental targets been established?
- ☐ Is there sufficient programme documentation?

Chapter 9
Operations

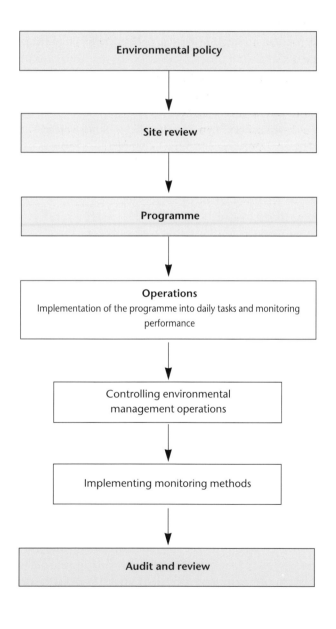

Environmental policy

Site review

Programme

Operations
Implementation of the programme into daily tasks and monitoring performance

Controlling environmental management operations

Implementing monitoring methods

Audit and review

Introduction

The previous sections of the EMS have determined the overall environmental aims of the organization, reviewed the current situation of the site and the ability of the organization to deal with environmental issues. On the basis of this information the organization has prepared a programme of actions to take. This chapter will show how and when to implement this programme. Implementing a programme means translating it into a sequence of projects and tasks scheduled according to the programme requirements and the organization's ability to undertake them.

The three basic requirements of the operations element of an EMS are as follows. It is necessary, first, to execute the programme; second, to monitor environmental performance; and third, to ensure that external auditors have evidence to assess the process and outcomes. Although many tourism sites have already informal operating systems in place, implementing an EMS usually means that some changes need to be made in the day-to-day management practices, procedures and processes. The outcomes of the operations element are documented evidence of:

- Resources allocated to environmental management projects and specific tasks.
- Projects and tasks sequenced and scheduled to take place.
- Projects carefully planned with consultation.
- Operating procedures in place.
- Monitoring that projects and tasks are undertaken.
- Facilities are inspected and maintained.
- Environmental management is assessed against the programme of actions.
- Environmental performance is assessed against targets and site review measurements.

Controlling environmental management operations

Every organization involved in tourism and recreation in the countryside will be already carrying out tasks, in a more or less orderly manner, and will use different terminology and forms. It is imperative for an EMS that tasks are somehow formalized to ensure quality and consistency. Since a site's operations will usually involve more people than any other element of an EMS, some organizations find it difficult to formalize their day-to-day routines to comply with an EMS. Four examples of operational control are further explained: allocation of resources, timing of projects, planning of projects, and introduction of procedures.

Allocating resources

Translating the actions agreed in the programme into projects and tasks to be carried out on a day-to-day basis will involve allocating resources to ensure environmental targets are met. Human, physical and financial resources need to be allocated to tasks to ensure they can be carried out, and evidence of the allocations should be stored in file.

Skills needed for each project and action need to be identified and responsibilities allocated for each specific task, either to members of staff or to external contractors. If the latter is the case, management needs to ensure that contractors comply with the organization's environmental policy. These responsibilities should be defined, explained and documented. A list of individuals involved in managing the environment and those that can affect the environment by doing their daily jobs should be completed: this will help to establish training requirements.

Materials needed to undertake the actions should be listed, with specific requirements, and the cost of them recorded. This will be linked to the organization's system of inventories, purchases and payments of materials, so it is crucial that the person dealing with purchasing is aware of the environmental requirements of materials. Once the type and amount of materials required have been listed, it is important to consider which tools will be needed to carry out the actions.

The cost of undertaking each task needs to be calculated in order to establish a budget for each project. Adjustments may need to be made according to the funds available and the feasibility of the programme reassessed. If unfeasible, it may be necessary to make amendments to the tasks, seek external contributions in kind or funding, or find other internal resources. Finance is an extremely important factor, as an organization can only do what they have funds for. But the whole EMS should be planned with available funds in mind. It is not sensible to prepare a grand programme and not be able to achieve it for lack of funds, since this may be an indication that the management system is not working well.

Sequencing and scheduling projects

The programme will need to be organized into a timetable showing when projects and tasks will be carried out. In order to do so, the manager will have to look at the sequence of tasks to determine what needs doing first, for future tasks to take place on time, and what length of time should be left between tasks. Tasks will also need to be scheduled according to the seasons and weather constraints, to ensure best growth of vegetation and also to avoid conflict with users.

The programme actions should be organized into lists of tasks with dates of when they can be done. Scheduling daily, weekly and monthly tasks and allocating tasks to staff can be done according to the organization's usual practice, but for the purpose of an EMS, records should be kept. A good way of doing it is to use a collective wall diary where weekly duties can be outlined. If another method is used to keep records of the tasks, it is good practice to keep a copy in a prominent place, where it is readily available to be consulted when work is under way.

Workloads will then need to be taken into account and some tasks might need to be re-scheduled. Since recreation and tourism are very seasonal, usually concentrated on weekends and in summer time, it may be important to plan out tasks that need to be done at certain times of the day, or days of the week, so as not to interfere with users. In general, most conservation activities will take place on weekdays, allowing recreation to continue at weekends; but this depends on the size of the operation. While operations are carried out, it is imperative that the health and safety of visitors is taken into account and that areas where building work or tree felling are taking place are fenced off from visitors. Where work is carried out on footpaths, alternative routes should be arranged and signposted.

Planning projects

Once tasks have been allocated, sequenced and scheduled, project planning forms can be used to bring together information relevant to the tasks to be carried out. Project planning forms are used as communication tools between those planning and those doing the tasks. Forms will vary from organization to organization and depending on the tasks. As an example, Case Study 9.1 shows some of the headings that could be in a project planning form for project leaders in volunteer work. In this case study, emphasis is placed on the health and safety of the participants, but at the same time environmental issues can be incorporated.

Ad hoc team work requires careful planning of materials, tools and supervision. This group of volunteers is restoring a pond to encourage a biodiversity focus

CASE STUDY 9.1

Project leader checklist of tasks

Once a member of staff has been made responsible to carry out a task, he or she ought to visit the site in advance and make an assessment of the task. Comments could be added to the project planning form on the following areas:

- *Materials.* Are suitable local materials available? List the type and amount of material needed, making sure you don't underestimate.
- *Tools needed.* A checklist of tools and equipment that they need for each task will be necessary. Previously made lists can be used.
- *Users.* Will it be used by individuals or groups, children or adults, cyclists or walkers; and depending on the users, do we have to adapt what we are doing?
- *Site review results and programme objectives.* What are the reasons this project was considered necessary? Are these obvious when visiting the site?
- *Usage wear and tear.* What is the highest usage likely to be? What do similar places look like? For example, if we are to build a gate, are there any other gates in the area, and do they suffer from something we can learn from?
- *Environmental wear and tear.* What is the worst weather likely to be? Will there be drainage or lack of water problems?
- *Seasonality of tasks.* While tasks like walling and fencing are possible any time, others, like footpath construction, tree felling or habitat management, are more specific to some times of the year.

Tools and equipment list for building fences:

- First-aid kit
- Gloves
- Fencing gauntlets
- Goggles
- Safety helmets
- Spirit levels
- Lines and pegs
- Tape measure
- Wire cutters
- Fencing pliers
- Surform
- Crowbar/pinch bar
- Wrecking bar/swan neck
- Drivall
- Tamper or punner
- Claw hammer
- Mallet
- Wood chisel
- Spades
- Shuvholers
- Bowsaw
- Mell or maul
- Wire stainers
- Stob holder
- Wire twister
- Staple extractor

Ensure all team members are wearing appropriate footwear and clothing and issue specified safety equipment

Source: BTCV, 36 St Mary's Street, Wallingford, Oxon OX10 0EU

Some organizations will already have systems in place where tasks to be carried out are communicated through forms. This may be for financial reasons, for documented evidence for an EMS, or where they have to be scrutinized internally or externally for other reasons. Table 9.1. shows what a project planning form could look like. Each cell in the form is referenced and its meaning outlined.

Table 9.1   Project planning form

Project code[1] and title[2]				
Project leader[3]	Priority[4]		Photograph[5]	
Work days[6]	Start date[6]		End date[6]	
Area/zone[7]			Special designation status[8]	
Description of task/s[9]				
Materials[10]	No. needed	In stock/purchase	Price per unit	Total cost
Equipment[11]				
Staff[12]				
Expenditure[13] Code Total		Income[13] Code Total		
Internal consultation[14]				
Stakeholders consultation[15]				
Text/comments[16]				

1. *Project code.* This is an individual way of identifying each project, which will be used to link the project to the overall environmental management system.
2. *Project title.* Name given to the overall project that this task or set of tasks is part of.
3. *Project leader.* The name of the person in charge of operations
4. *Priority.* Some organizations will define different levels of priority, and code them in their own way. For example, operations could be prioritized from one to four, as compulsory/recommended/advisable, or by when they should be done (1/5/15 days).
5. *Photograph.* Where applicable, managers may want to keep a record of pictures of the work carried out. This is a practical way of clarifying operations and minimizing details when writing forms. This box will be marked Y or N depending on whether pictures are requested, or it could indicate the number and type of pictures wanted.
6. *Timing.* The planned duration in work days will be established, and the project will be allocated a start date and end date.
7. *Area/zone.* The site will have previously been divided into differentiated areas, and this box will be used to define in which areas work will take place.
8. *Special conservation designation.* If extra environmental protection measures have to be observed, this will be noted.
9. *Description of the task/s.* An outline of the work that needs to be carried out on the ground.
10. *Materials.* It is imperative to have a list of the material that will be necessary, and this should have been listed after assessment on the site. Special emphasis should be placed on material that needs to be bought for the task, and costs recorded on the expenditure cells.
11. *Equipment.* Equipment needed will be listed, noting any equipment that is either not available on site or that needs to be booked for this activity.
12. *Staff.* Staff responsible and number of staff involved will be recorded.
13. *Finance.* If this activity incurs some expenditure or potential income, amounts will be included here and codes from the organizational budgets will be added. This will make each task more easily accountable.
14. *Internal consultation.* The person planning a project should pass on this form to other people that might be affected or can benefit from the operations, and their suggestions recorded in the form.
15. *External consultation.* Organizations or individuals that might be affected outside the organization should be consulted and comments recorded.
16. *Text/comments.* Finally there will be a section to allow the person planning the project to add any specific details on how the task has to be done, i.e. any differences from previous occasions or important issues to take into account. This box will be used for non-routine jobs or for those with special requirements.

Introducing operating procedures

Project planning forms provide the organization with evidence that the project has been thought out before being undertaken. Now it is necessary to ensure that tasks are carried out correctly. All operations with a potential impact on the environment need to have clear, documented procedures stating the sequence of actions and how these should be taken. Procedures can be used as quality assurance methods, by providing a consistent approach to dealing with environmental issues. Procedures can be quite simple and relate to day-to-day activities, and they can either be formal documents or the result of unwritten but accepted work practice. Yet to be successful and effective, a procedure should be understandable, actionable, auditable and mandatory.

Procedures are required both for regular tasks and for emergency situations too, so that everyone knows exactly what to do if there is a major incident. Emergency procedures are useful methods of dealing with something that goes wrong, or if a specific accident happens and a quick decision must be taken. It is already normal for organizations to have procedures related to health and safety, such as what to do when there is a work accident or a fire alarm. Environmental procedures will follow similar structures and apply them to their particular setting. For example, if recreation and tourism sites in countryside locations are in an area of fire risk, they will have to implement fire prevention and fire management procedures.

In small organizations, especially those where few staff are involved in paperwork, information is usually kept in the manager's office or the staff room. Larger companies may keep more than one copy of each procedure so staff have a copy for reference, while there is still one copy in the manager's room for record and also to ensure that neither contradiction nor omission takes place. In any case, organizations must make sure that all staff involved in a task have access to the procedures that relate to it.

Case Study 9.2. is an example of a procedure that has brought success to the rangers of Burnham Beeches in stopping cyclists riding off-road.

It is important to implement procedures to the internal communication methods in organizations where different people are in charge of recreation, conservation and agricultural/timber production. This is especially relevant for non-routine activities, since these can cause unexpected disturbance to other users. For example, if tree felling is due, the person in charge of organizing it will have to communicate internally the intention to fell a certain number of trees in a defined area and a date. This gives the conservation officer and the recreation officer an opportunity to comment on the suitability of the proposal. From a conservation point of view, the officer might be concerned that tree felling in a certain place may affect a certain type of birds nesting in the area, and suggest felling similar trees in another place where this would create a forest clearing to encourage butterflies. The recreation officer may agree with the forest clearing, but might prefer it starts on a Monday and it is finished before the weekend, rather than starting mid-week and leaving machinery on site over a busy weekend of visitors.

CASE STUDY 9.2

Using procedures to manage off-road cycling

Site review

Burnham Beeches is situated close to London and a number of large local towns. It is a National Nature Reserve and public open space owned and managed by the Corporation of London. The site covers an area of 220 hectares and is visited by approximately 500,000 people each year, and therefore this is a heavily used site. Notable habitats within the site are wood pasture, heath, wetland and open water. Of particular importance to the site are the 500 ancient beech pollards.

In recent years there has been an increase in off-road mountain bike use and the rangers have identified the following impacts: soil erosion, danger to other visitors, conflict with other user groups, wildlife disturbance, destruction of plants and their habitats, noise, construction of obstacles, litter, and infringement of Corporation bylaws.

Programme

Off-road cycling was identified by the management as an area of concern, and a meeting was arranged to suggest solutions. The result was the implementation of an off-road cycling policy. Managing off-road cyclists was given a high priority and resources were allocated. Dates and responsibilities for planned actions were agreed.

Operations

The rangers were given the task to 'Actively approach all off-road cyclists'. A series of actions were designed to assist them, ensuring all relevant user groups were targeted. The following actions were among those to be implemented as part of this policy:

- Production of occasional articles in existing newsletter to reinforce the 'no off-road cycling' message.
- Production of an 'off-road cycling' leaflet/windscreen flyer.
- Production of a dedicated display for the Information Unit.
- Increase patrols at busy periods, e.g. during school holidays.
- Establish contact with the mountain bike press.
- Erect 'No cycling' signs at problem areas.
- Erect new gate closing signs incorporating the 'No off road cycling' message.

The following procedure has been written to ensure consistency when members of staff approach off-road cyclists:

- Where can visitors cycle off the roads? It is important to make it clear that off-road cycling is not allowed in any part of the site.
- Who do we approach? All off-road cyclists with the exception of when mum and dad are on foot escorting their young children who are on bikes.
- When do we approach? 365 days of the year. If the cyclists are seen riding off-road it is our duty to approach them.
- Where do we approach? Effort must be made to target the problem areas where it is a common assumption that it is OK to cycle here.
- How effective will this be? The policy will take at least a year to show positive results but by structuring the approach will ensure that the message is difficult to miss. One single lax patrol could weaken the effectiveness of the policy.
- When will we have additional patrols?

These will be carried out during school holidays and at weekends.

- What if the situation starts to get heated? We do not want to alienate any of our visitors but some level of verbal conflict is possible. As long as we carry out our duty in a professional, polite and technically correct manner we will be able to reduce any conflict and start to make a difference. If necessary, walk away from a situation rather than allow an argument to develop.
- When do we start? Direct approaches to off-road cyclists should commence on 1 January 1998.

- Monitoring? A specific monitoring form has been designed for recording off-road cycling numbers, approaches made, time, date and location. It is important that records are kept so that the effect of this policy can be accurately assessed.
- Trial Period. The year 2000 should be seen as one in which we test our procedures. Refinements are almost inevitable and should be brought to the attention of the Head Keeper as they are identified.

Based on the procedure, staff will fill in the following recording sheet.

Date	AM/PM	No. Seen	No. Spoken to	Where	Recorded by	Comments
21/02/98	AM	3	3	Dell car park	R. Marston	Flyers issued
21/02/98	PM	4	4	Morton Drive	R. Marston	Flyers issued

Source: Burnham Beeches, Hawthorn Lane, Farnham Common, Slough SL2 3TE

Example of 'No cycling' sign

Procedures can also be used to deal with events organized by groups from outside the organization that will use the site (e.g. mountain bike competitions, orienteering exercises, organized walks). An event permission form should be filled in by a representative of the group organizing the event, and this form should have room for different people in the company to make comments as to the suitability of such an event and recommendations for change, should this be necessary.

Implementing monitoring methods

Every organization should check their progress to ensure the desired outcome is achieved, and to ensure no unforeseen problems have occurred. Monitoring is the process of comparing environmental performance measurements, and it is necessary for the following reasons:

- *To keep track of progress.* To ensure that the activities planned happened when expected and that the programme targets are being met
- *To keep track of results.* To ensure that actions are actually producing the desired results
- *To encourage participants.* By displaying results and progress, feedback can be provided, and encouragement and recognition given to those involved in implementing the EMS, demonstrating that their efforts are paying off.

An EMS places a strong emphasis on keeping records of actions to ensure these can be assessed in the future, both internally and externally. The monitoring systems within the company will have to fulfil four purposes. First, they will ensure actions are recorded as they take place, since they are hard to do retrospectively as they relate to the situation on the ground at specific times. This should be part of day-to-day tasks for the organization. Second, they will make possible that measuring records should be maintained and stored carefully so that they can be found easily when required. Third, measurements should be simple and understandable, comparable across time, able to show progress being made and track changes rigorously and honestly. Fourth, the monitoring procedures will establish a procedure for conducting an internal audit and review, including when it will be updated and how the findings will be followed up.

A site will have its environmental performance and environmental management monitored in three ways. First, project recording forms will ensure that tasks outlined in the programme are carried out. Second, the site will have a plan of environmental performance surveys. Third, facility maintenance forms will provide evidence that the site is well kept for visitors and that potential environmental hazards are managed. From these three sources of evidence the organization will write an environmental monitoring report that will provide evidence of the overall environmental performance and environmental management system which will be used as a key document for the audit and review element of the EMS.

Monitoring the effects of tourism and recreation in the countryside will vary according to the nature of the tasks carried out. To see the results of a horticultural plan, it may take three to five years; in woodlands it could be ten to twenty years, yet only a few months to see the differences in amenity or visitor management. Case Study 9.3 shows some of the components of a bird migration monitoring plan in Portugal. Although the individual cycles will vary depending on what is managed, an overall EMS monitoring plan will usually consist of a pre-defined number of measurements per week, month, year or management cycle, for each type of information that should be collected.

CASE STUDY 9.3

Bird migration monitoring plan

Programme
The Natural Reserve of Dunas de S. Jacinto in Portugal carries out research on bird migration. One of the project's objectives is to get more information about these birds' behaviour and about the way they use and move through the area. Results have also been used to determine recreation activity, space and time zoning necessary to accomplish the site's preservation commitment.

Operations
The site's management staff and the investigation project technicians had defined a monitoring plan that included:

- The responsible technician.
- The staff involved: an ornithologist and two forest guards. The guards will get training while helping in the initial monitoring actions. This will permit the monitoring process continuing after the investigation project end.
- The monitoring object: the project will focus on the duck populations, especially the Royal Duck (*Anas platyrhynchos*).
- The monitoring procedures: internationally recognized metal ring application, nasal marks, radio-emitter installation, captured animals' parameters and rangefinder data registration.
- Register parameters: species, metal ring code, sex, age, weight, measures (wing, beak, finger, etc.).
- Work field-days schedule.
- Necessary equipment.
- The data treatment process.

Source: Delegação de Coimbra do ICN, Mata Nacional do Choupal, 3000 Coimbra, Portugal

---

Project recording forms

Records should be maintained to demonstrate compliance with the requirements of the EMS and the extent to which the objectives and targets are met. Project recording forms could be used to complement the project planning forms. These will either be similar so comparisons can be made, or the same form will be used to plan and record results by adding a few more cells. Table 9.2 can be used to keep a record of any potential deviations from the plan and the reasons behind such changes. In the case of a project recording form, the cells will be used to write down how things actually took place, so comparisons can be drawn.

Taking pictures of the site before, during and after the work is done will provide evidence of the improvement. Initially this was a highly eroded stop caused by visitors approaching the lake. Building this duck-board minimized shore impacts

Table 9.2   Project recording form

Project code and title				
Recorder				
Date of record completion	Project status		Photograph	
Work days	Start date		End date	
Area/zone			Special designation status	
Description of task/s				
Materials	No. needed	In stock/purchase	Price per unit	Total cost
Equipment				
Staff				
Expenditure Code Total		Income Code Total		
Text/comments				

Environmental performance surveys

An overall plan of environmental performance surveys should list and date measurements to take evidence about the current situation. The only way to see if targets have been met or if progress towards these targets is being made is to measure the significant impact, again using the same measuring technique as before, as already discussed in the site review. By taking further measurements regularly, it is possible to assess the effectiveness of the actions chosen to alleviate the significant impact. The person taking records should use the same measuring technique in similar conditions to ensure consistency, or if the conditions are different this should be noted. All recordings that are necessary for the monitoring plan will be collected by a project register.

Facility maintenance surveys

Each site will have to check regularly the maintenance of recreation facilities to ensure that health and safety standards are kept and that potential environmental impacts are controlled. Use and wear and tear will determine how often each facility needs to be checked, and while some footpaths will only need to be inspected three times a year, interpretation boards might need monthly checking and toilets daily.

Regular inspections of the footpaths will ensure that these are maintained. In this section of the path, the inspector would check that the steps are safe and that people are not widening the path outside the designated area

Facility maintenance forms (Table 9.3) can be used to ensure that all the facilities are checked and records are kept. In the case of a footpath, for example, the form will include all waymarks and signs, the path surface, any hazardous objects on the path verge, and any other items specific to the footpath. If appropriate, a map of the area can be included with the form to locate each item that needs checking. Any defects will be noted and prioritized, indicating when the job needs to be done on an urgency scale. This could range from 1 to 5, 1 meaning that it needs sorting within the day, 2 within a week, 3 within a month, 4 within three months, and 5 within six months. Each facility will need a different form since inspections will be carried out at different times and potentially by different people.

Table 9.3 Facility inspection form

Facility name Visitor Centre footpath 1 (blue route) Checked by Date Last date inspected					
Description	*Location code*	*Defect*	*Action*	*Urgency*	*Date completed*
Start sign	S1				
Start map	S2				
Warning signs	W1				
	W2				
Waymarkers	WM1				
	WM2				
	WM3				
	WM4				
Roadcross signs	R1				
Benches	B1				
	B2				
Cliff fence	C1				
Trail surface	TS				

Source: Forest Enterprise, 231 Costorphine Rd., Edinburgh, EH12 7AT

Sites can use the same maintenance form to check when tasks are completed, as in the example, where the person carrying out the maintenance writes in the date it was completed and inserts his or her initials next to it. When activities involve several people, it may be convenient to draw a monthly recreation maintenance plan of activities, with dates to start and complete each task, number of hours and the cost.

Environmental monitoring report

The environmental manager will be able to write an overall environmental monitoring report using the previous information to produce two environmental monitoring forms.

The organization will have to monitor the management process followed to achieve that environmental performance (Table 9.4). This will be done by using information relating to the project recording forms, indicating whether the actions and tasks suggested in the programme were operationalized, and commenting on the particular conditions that influenced the organization's actions. If the results achieved differ from those expected, the environmental assessor can track the reasons back to the documents relating to the planning of the projects. This information can then be compared against the current environmental management practice report produced in the site review stage.

Environmental performance surveys will produce up-to-date measurements of the environmental performance that can be compared against previous recordings (Table 9.5). It will compare the measurements after carrying out the operations with the site review measurements and the targets set in the programme. Comments for the reasons for the actual result, in comparison with the initial measurement and the target, should be stated.

Outcomes

Carrying out the environmental management operations will result in an environmental monitoring report, divided into two sections. First, an assessment of the environmental management of the site, based on the evidence provided by the records of the implementation of the environmental programme and the monitoring of projects and facilities. Second, an assessment of the environmental performance, based on the continuous measurement of significant environmental impacts and comparing the readings at the site review operations stages against programme targets. This places the organization in a prime position to audit and review the EMS.

Table 9.4 Summary of monitoring report – environmental management

Prioritized significant impact	Action/Actions	Operations completed Y/N	Initials	date	Comments on operations
Pollution from anglers	Provide bins	Y	RV	05/02	Three new bins have been placed at maximum use points
	Indicate on maps where the bins can be found	N			Maps will not be updated until following year
	Provide signs directing users to bins	Y	SG	08/02	Signs have been erected
	Educate visitors to take their litter home	Y	RV	Ongoing	Code of Conduct printed on back of fishing permit
	Reduce packaging on sold goods	Y	SG	15/03	Sandwiches are sold without plastic packaging
Footpath soil damage	Re-route footpath	Y	KY	17/03	Footpaths re-routed but not changed on site map
	Pinch-point unofficial footpaths	Y	RV	22/03	Log pinch-points placed at start of unofficial footpaths
	Replace topsoil	Y	RV	03/04	Heavy rain the day after topsoil replaced washed it all away
Habitat change along footpaths	Pinch-point large and vulnerable trees	Y	JT	05/04	Pinch-points are being used as rest places, still habitat change
	Pinch-point diversions	Y	SG	22/03	Successful for bicycles, not for pedestrians
	Introduce penalty for anyone found vandalizing trees	N	SG	09/04	Penalty agreed as site ban, but not enforced at present
	Introduce signposts	Y	RV	16/04	Ten signposts erected, two of which vandalized
	Introduce guided tours and self-guided tours	N			Recruitment advert to be placed in local paper in near future
Congestion of local roads	Visitor survey and analysis	Y	Student	01/10	4,000 cars counted during peak season 67 per cent of visitors travel under twelve miles to each site 85 per cent of visitors preferred to use own car than public transport Visitors prepared to pay more for car parking
Disturbance of nesting sparrow hawk	Pinch-point the nest	Y	RV	22/03	Pinch-pointing has brought visitor attention
	Provide remote view of the nest via a camera	Y	JT	25/10	Pressure removed. Revenue from showing video of chicks

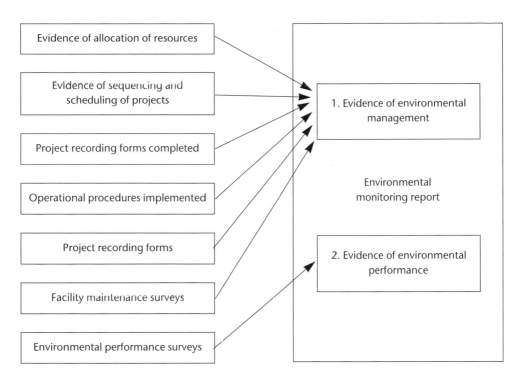

Figure 9.1 Summary of operations outcomes

Checklist

☐ Is there evidence of allocation of resources to environmental tasks and projects?
☐ Is there evidence of the sequencing and scheduling of environmental tasks and projects?
☐ Does the organization use some formalized form to plan environmental projects?
☐ Are environmentally sensitive actions communicated internally and externally?
☐ Are there procedures to operationalize the programme?
☐ Are staff aware of environmentally related procedures?
☐ Is evidence of operations and procedures kept up to date and available?
☐ Are the results of environmental projects recorded?
☐ Are environmental performance surveys carried out regularly?
☐ Are facilities inspected regularly and deficiencies dealt with?
☐ Does the organization have an up-to-date environmental monitoring report?
☐ Are operations implementing all the programme's projects and actions?
☐ Are all significant impacts monitored?
☐ Are all results from operations monitored?
☐ Are results from operations monitored against the programme targets?
☐ Are results from operations monitored against the site review measurements?
☐ Is there an environmental management monitoring report?
☐ Is there an environmental performance monitoring report?

Table 9.5 Summary of monitoring report – environmental performance

Prioritized significant impacts	Probable causes	Measurement method	Site review measurement	Programme environment target	Operations measurement	Comments on performance
Pollution from anglers	Lack of care and concern from some site users. Lack of warning signs promoting the issues. No policing of the area. No rubbish bins near the river	Volume of waste collected from fishing area over six-week period. Problem area located on map	32 sacks of litter picked up from fishing area	To reduce pollution from anglers by 50 per cent in twelve months	Eighteen sacks over the same period	Targets were not achieved because there was an increase in visitors to the area. Overall results considered very positive by management
Footpath soil damage	Trampling and compaction from too many visitors over-using particular sections	Site survey: checklist identifying problem areas and severity, carried out by student. Key areas photographed and highlighted on map	Four problem areas, one of which is very severe. Damaged area 24m². One in the conservation area, damage 12m²	To reduce footpath soil damage by 20 per cent in 24 months	No change in three areas. Impacts were eradicated in the conservation area	Temporarily diverting walkers from conservation area achieved the results expected, however actions had little effect in other areas. Visitors ignoring log pinch-points
Habitat change along footpaths	Vandalism has risen, especially to trees, with the increase in visitors. Paths are not maintained regularly. Deterioration causes users to create diversions. Lack of interpretation about conservation areas, therefore visitors may not be aware they are walking through a special area	Site survey: identifying habitat zones, carried out by student. Key areas photographed and highlighted on map	Two problem areas highlighted. Heathland verges invaded by bracken. Ash avenue, twenty saplings, eleven showed other damage	To reduce habitat change along footpaths by 25 per cent in twelve months	Bracken reduced by 30 per cent. Damage to ash reduced by 15 per cent	Sheep grazing has reduced bracken spread but also has badly affected ash regeneration. Use of the footpath where ash is situated has doubled causing 34 broken ash saplings and twenty showing other damage

Congestion of local roads	Not known	Not applicable	Not applicable	To identify how the site contributes to the congestion of local roads within one year	4,000 cars counted during peak season. 67 per cent of visitors travel under twelve miles to reach site. 85 per cent of visitors preferred to use own car than public transport. Visitors prepared to pay more for car parking	Two of the three weekends that the survey was carried out on were extremely wet which meant that only 450 visitors surveyed. Student who carried out survey inexperienced in questionnaire design
Disturbance of nesting sparrow hawk	Visitors are allowed too close to the nest	Count of sparrow-hawk population numbers. Count of young reaching maturity. Expert opinion used	Four pairs in spring 1990. Two pairs in spring 1999 and five young reached maturity	To eradicate disturbance in six months	Four pairs in 2,000. Four of the five young that reached maturity still alive, two of which have mated	One sparrow hawk found run over. Especially good year for small mammals meaning a good supply of prey for the sparrow hawks

Chapter 10

Audit and Review

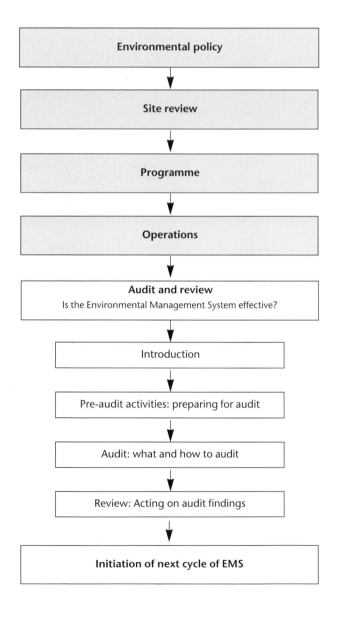

Environmental policy

Site review

Programme

Operations

Audit and review
Is the Environmental Management System effective?

Introduction

Pre-audit activities: preparing for audit

Audit: what and how to audit

Review: Acting on audit findings

Initiation of next cycle of EMS

Introduction

The purpose of audit and review is to conduct a regular and systematic evaluation of the EMS. Audit and review are distinct but closely related processes.

The main concern of an audit is to establish exactly what has taken place. The audit should focus on two key aspects of the EMS. Its first priority is to determine the effectiveness of the management system itself and therefore record the structure and workings of that system, with particular reference to its proficiency in delivering environmental improvement. Its second priority is to report on how well the environmental policy and programme have been carried out, and specifically on whether targets have been met. Audit is therefore concerned with the performance of the management system and the environmental performance of the site.

The main concern of the review is to 'close the loop' in the EMS. The information collected by the audit is assessed to determine if corrective action is needed. Review should be carried out at a senior level in the organization. It should focus on two key questions:

1. How are areas for concern raised by the audit to be addressed and followed up?
2. How will the review findings be incorporated into the next cycle of the EMS?

This chapter considers the tasks to be addressed before, during and after the audit. The whole process is illustrated in Figure 10.1

There are three stages to the process of audit and review:

1. Pre-audit activities.
2. Audit.
3. Review.

It is important to emphasize that audit and review are not the end of the EMS process. Since the EMS process is continual and cyclical, initiation of next cycle of the EMS should also be considered.

Pre-audit activities

The procedure for the audit should have already been established during the operations phase of the EMS. This should have covered:

1. who will be responsible for developing the audit process;
2. how often will auditing occur;
3. the budget for the audit;
4. what the contents of the audit report will be;
5. access to relevant documents and records;
6. access to staff for interviews;
7. how the audit report will be used.

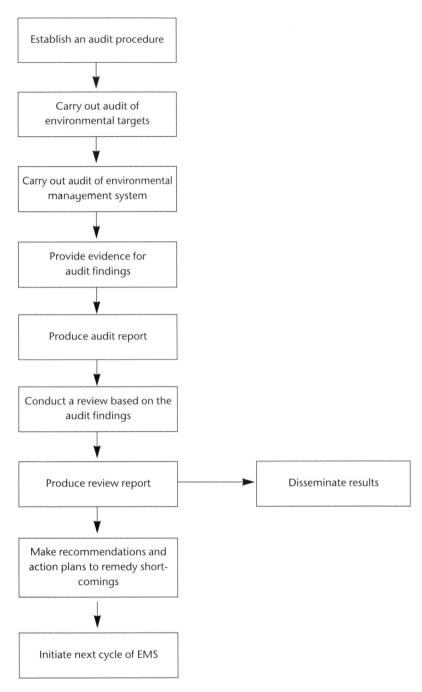

Figure 10.1 The audit and review process

The quality of an audit depends on who is implementing it and their experience. Whoever carries it out should be properly trained for the task. In some cases, this may mean that external specialists are called upon, but in many cases the necessary auditing skills may be found internally. However, if these were developed in areas such as quality control or finance, it must be ensured that skills are adapted to cater for environmental issues. Developing a team of auditors from different areas within the organization may be necessary to achieve the breadth and experience required for an audit team.

Audit

The main objectives of the audit are to:

1. determine whether the environmental management system is effective (management);
2. check environmental performance against stated targets outlined in the policy and programme (environmental performance);
3. check that significant environmental impacts are being addressed.

The International Chamber of Commerce (ICC) defined an environmental audit as:

A management tool comprising a systematic, documented, periodic and objective evaluation of how well environmental organization, management and equipment are performing with the aim of helping to safeguard the environment by (i) facilitating management control of environmental practices; (ii) assessing compliance with company policies, which would include meeting regulatory requirements.

David Russell, Head of Forestry for the National Trust, explains its purpose as:

. . . using the indicators set in the plan to assess the effectiveness of actions in meeting objectives over time. My job, and that of my advisory colleagues, has a major component of auditing and finding the best means to deal with the weaknesses exposed by audit. (Font and Tribe, 2000)

An EMS audit should be a regular event. Its frequency will be determined by the length of the EMS cycle. It should be a systematic and documented check. The objectives of the audit must be established at the outset to limit and focus audit activities, otherwise it may be found that a disproportionate amount of time is spent on one objective at the expense of others. The specific requirements of the audit will be unique to individual sites and will depend on the size and complexity of the site and organization.

Audit documentation does not have a pre-defined structure. The format best suited to an individual organization should be followed. If there is a defined structure for other audits such as quality control or finance, they may be adapted easily for the purpose of the EMS.

Creating a checklist of items to audit helps to keep track of progress and provides a simple guide to follow. Table 10.1 is an example of a checklist containing items that have been generated from previous sections of the EMS. Note that there is one additional section, Programme (as identified for particular site). This will be the programme of environmental targets that have been identified by a management team to address the needs of their site and will therefore be site-specific.

Table 10.1   Audit checklist

Audit item	Outcome Y/N/NA	Evidence and location
Policy		
Is there a written policy document?		
Has the policy been formulated using stakeholder involvement?		
Does the policy show commitment to continued environmental improvement?		
Is there a commitment to comply with environmental legislation?		
Is there a commitment to manage activities with significant environmental impacts?		
Is there a commitment to educate stakeholders about environmental issues?		
Is there a commitment to ensure that suppliers and user groups contribute to environmental policy?		
Is the policy written in clear and understandable language?		
Does the policy identify all significant issues?		
Has the policy been endorsed at the highest management level?		
Is the policy integrated into the organization's main mission/policy statement?		
Has the policy been disseminated to staff?		
Are staff aware of the commitments made in the environmental policy?		
Has the policy been disseminated to other stakeholders?		
Is there an agreed date for review?		
Is the purpose of having a policy understood?		
Site review		
Is responsibility for carrying out the review assigned?		
Has previous work relevant to the review been identified?		
Have start and finish times been selected?		

Audit item	Outcome Y/N/NA	Evidence and location
Is the environmental policy giving direction to the review?		
Has the current management framework of the site been assessed?		
Is there a report on current environmental management practice?		
Has the status of procedures for legislation been investigated?		
Is there a background to the site report?		
Is there a profile report for recreational activities?		
Have the environmental impacts of recreation activities to the site been identified?		
Has a procedure been developed for identifying which impacts are significant?		
Have the significant impacts for the site been identified and assessed?		
Can the significant impacts be measured?		
Have appropriate methods of measurement been identified and used?		
Is there a register of significant impacts and related activities and a baseline measurement?		
Programme (management)		
Has the current environmental management report been assessed?		
Has the organization got a strong environmental culture?		
Is environmental management included in the organization's structure?		
Are there environmental management systems in place to ensure that environmental management is carried out?		
Has an environmental champion been chosen?		
Is there an environmental management manual?		
Are environmental responsibilities, tasks and duties defined in job descriptions?		
Is there environmental training available for those that require it?		
Has a programme for environmental management system been established and implemented?		
Have significant impacts been prioritized?		
Has the prioritization process been justified?		
Have environmental targets been set?		
Have questions been asked to ensure that the actions selected are successful?		
Has a programme to meet environmental targets been established?		
Is there sufficient programme documentation?		

Audit item	Outcome Y/N/NA	Evidence and location
Programme (as identified for your site)		
Have you achieved environmental target . . .		
1.		
2.		
3.		
4.		
5.		
6.		
7.		
8.		
Operations		
Is there evidence of allocation of resources to environmental tasks and projects?		
Is there evidence of the sequencing and scheduling of environmental tasks and projects?		
Does the organization use some formalized form to plan environmental projects?		
Are environmentally sensitive actions communicated internally and externally?		
Are there procedures to operationalize the programme?		
Are staff aware of environmentally related procedures?		
Is evidence of operations and procedures kept up to date and available?		
Are the results of environmental projects recorded?		
Are environmental performance surveys carried out regularly?		
Are facilities inspected regularly and deficiencies dealt with?		
Does the organization have an up to date environmental monitoring report?		
Are operations implementing all the programme's projects and actions?		
Are all significant impacts monitored?		
Are all results from operations monitored?		
Are results from operations monitored against the programme targets?		
Are results from operations monitored against the site review measurements?		
Is there an environmental management monitoring report?		
Is there an environmental performance monitoring report?		

Audit item	Outcome Y/N/NA	Evidence and location
Audit and review		
Has an audit and review procedure been established?		
Does the audit assess all the components of the EMS?		
Does the audit assess environmental performance against stated targets?		
Does the audit assess the EMS itself?		
Is evidence provided to underpin claims of the EMS?		
Has an audit report been completed?		
Will senior management review the audit?		
Has a review report been completed?		
Does the review report summarize the main findings of the audit and recommendations arising from it?		
Is an action plan produced to follow up review recommendations?		

An essential requirement for an audit is not just the checking of achievements but also the need to indicate what evidence exists for claims that are being made. This is particularly important if the organization is seeking external validation of their EMS. External reviewers will want to be satisfied that claims for management systems and environmental improvement can be substantiated.

Table 10.2 shows examples of evidence and how it can be recorded.

Table 10.2 Examples of audit and evidence

Audit item	Outcome Y/N/NA	Evidence
Policy		
Is there a written policy document?	Y	Written policy
Has the policy been formulated using stakeholder involvement?	Y	Minutes of meetings
Is the policy integrated into the organization's main mission/policy statement?	N	
Has the policy been endorsed at the highest management level?	Y	Minutes of meeting
Site review		
Is there a background to the site report?	Y	Report
Have the environmental impacts of recreation activities to the site been identified?	Y	Completed pro-formas
Programme		
Are environmental responsibilities, tasks and duties defined in job descriptions?	Y	Job descriptions checked and recorded at audit
Programme (as identified for your site)		
Have you achieved target . . .		
Encourage use of public transport	Y	Survey showing increase in visitors arriving by public transport
Improve fire risk awareness and fire fighting equipment	Y	Physical evidence

In some cases auditors can check physical evidence

Case Study 10.1 shows how a programme to introduce new signage and information boards in Montesinho (Portugal) was found on audit to have used inappropriate materials, leading to a review of the design specification.

A short report should be written to summarize the findings of the audit.

CASE STUDY 10.1

Montesinho (Portugal): using regional materials as a way to reduce maintenance costs

Programme
The ICN (Portuguese Institute for Nature Conservation) central services have a programme to introduce uniform signalling and information materials for every protected area. This model was introduced into the Montesinho Natural Park area.

Audit
Due to severe weather conditions the new boards very soon started to show signs of deterioration, needing maintenance or even replacement. The old signal and information boards that used regional materials were found to be much more resistant to the climate and so did not need maintenance for several years.

Review
New guidelines were produced in the light of the audit. These suggest the use of regional resources such as stone and wood on new infrastructures (e.g. signal and information posts, bus stops and others) in the park area. The recommended wood is that from the chestnut tree and the recommended regional stones are granite and schist. This means reducing costs for infrastructure maintenance and at the same time encouraging the use of local resources which helps to maintain the traditional look of things.

Source: Instituto da Conservação da Natureza (Parque Natural de Montesinho), Portugal

Deteriorating Information Board at Montesinho

Review

Barry Collins, Ecology Manager of Center Parcs (UK) explains the point of review in the EMS used by his organization as follows:

> . . . Finally we have the management review. This is the process of determining the success of the whole system and the actions required to address any shortfalls. This review has to be conducted by the very top of the organization, a deliberate requirement to ensure the system gets the support in order to keep it viable. (Font and Tribe, 2000)

The review meeting is the key to ensuring the effectiveness of the EMS. The EMS review should be conducted by a panel which sits formally in order to conduct its business. The purposes of the review are to assess the overall performance of the EMS and to programme any actions necessary to rectify problems identified by the audit process

Assessment of the overall performance of the EMS and action plan

The key documents needed to assess the performance of the EMS are the completed audit and checklist, and the EMS policy.

The outcome of this part of the review should be a report that summarizes the achievements of the EMS and the programme of environmental targets highlighting any necessary actions that need to be instigated. This report should contain the following:

- a summary of the audit process;
- a record of the names of the auditors;
- a short summary of the findings;

- the main achievements of the EMS;
- the main environmental targets achieved;
- the key shortcomings of the EMS;
- the environmental targets that have not been achieved;
- recommendations resulting from audit;
- an action plan;
- appendices containing relevant background details and any data.

Recommendations should provide clear and appropriate suggestions for action plans that need to be initiated as a result of audit and review. These will take into account the resources required and the length of time needed to implement changes. They should identify staff responsibilities and completion dates.

Consideration of the review report should be a standing agenda item for the executive of the organization, so that environmental management achieves equal status to other activities of the organization.

Some organizations may wish to publish the results of their review. For large organizations the EMS review may be communicated through their annual report. Smaller organizations may wish to inform the public by a press release or include the results of review in their newsletter.

Figure 10.2 provides a blank action plan that enables the progress of recommendations and associated follow-up actions to be monitored. The point of this document is to ensure that the recommendations that arise from audit and review are systematically followed up. For this reason a copy of the full action plan should be retained by the review panel and reviewed at its next meeting.

Case Study 10.2 describes the experimental introduction of a new species into a forest park in Portugal. It demonstrates how such an experiment can be incorporated into the various stages of an EMS. In particular, the operations section explains the use of monitoring techniques which were used in the audit to check the success and effects of the experiment. The review contains clear action points to improve the experiment in the future.

Initiation of next cycle of EMS

After the review process the organization should take steps to initiate the next round of the EMS cycle. The starting point for this should be a review of the appropriateness of the current policy. In order to start the next EMS cycle the following need to be available:

- The current policy.
- An overview of new and planned legislation.
- An understanding of emerging public environmental issues.
- An understanding of local community concerns.
- New environmental concerns from any area.

Recommendation	Action required	Responsibility	Deadline	Monitored by

Copies to:
    review panel
    staff responsible for action
    staff responsible for monitoring

Figure 10.2   Action sheet for review

CASE STUDY 10.2

Audit and review of the introduction of a new species (common squirrel) in Monsanto, Portugal

Site review

Monsanto's Ecological Park (PEM) is inside the Monsanto Forest Park, Lisbon's biggest green area. One of its objectives was to study the introduction and spread of the common squirrel (*Sciurus vulgaris infuscatus*). This species had probably previously existed in the forested areas of this region. A first group of fifteen squirrels was released in the PEM area. At the same time twelve artificial nests, five drinkers and one artificial feeder were established to avoid food shortages and to control the area used by the animals during the adaptation period.

Programme

Based on previous squirrel studies the programme set a target increase of 23 animals in the first year. It included a study of the adaptation and dispersion of the squirrel population and the option to release new animals if necessary. In addition it was decided to evaluate the animals' condition and the population's evolution and distribution in the PEM and the Forest Park area. For this a continuous field study was commissioned to:

*   conduct a census of animals inside and outside the park and locate the squirrels' selected territory;
*   analyse their dispersion reasons and strategies and identify their main source of nourishment;
*   study the population's dynamics, namely the interactions and possibly conflicts with other species;
*   study the importance of visitors and activities in the population's dynamic.

Operations

The implementation and monitoring methods were as follows.
Measurement methods:

*   Counting and map registration of squirrels. For this the methods used are direct observation of specimens and the presence of vestiges like food scraps or nests.
*   Identify the nests and do a continuous study of the surrounding area.
*   Analyse the needs and reactions to the artificial nests, feeders and drinkers.
*   Photographic record of the squirrels and their nests to help in individual identification.
*   Record of deaths, their causes and the study of each animal's parameters.

Study area: Monsanto's Forest Park, beginning in the PEM area.
Workdays: All year, three days per week.
Output: Monthly reports and maps.

Audit and review

After one year it was calculated that only about ten animals were still alive, which was much lower than the expected. The main causes were:

*   The male and female proportion was not probably the ideal one.
*   Some of the deaths happened between two procreation periods.
*   There were probably a greater number of deaths than the ones recorded.
*   The artificial amenities introduced were not located in the best position. For instance the nests should have been put in a higher position in the top of the trees.

- The number of artificial feeders should also be greater. The introduction of supplement food by the PEM staff and by visitors could also increase the number of animals.

In the review it was suggested that when introducing a new group of animals they should be released into a closed area during an initial period of two or three weeks. That would permit the animals to adapt to the area and to the artificial amenities. There must be better design and distribution of feeders, with at least one per two animals. A system of traps was also suggested to assist in monitoring.

Source: Parque Ecologico de Monsanto, Portugal

Figure 10.3 shows how the review process closes the loop of the EMS and leads into the next cycle of environmental management. This next cycle will entail revisions to policy and a new site review, and will instigate the next cycle of programme and operations. It is important to note that action plans arising from the previous cycle should be incorporated into the next cycle so that they are systematically followed up.

Outcomes

The outcomes of audit and review are:

- An audit report.
- A review report with recommendations and an action plan.

Checklist

☐ Has an audit and review procedure been established?
☐ Does the audit assess all the components of the EMS?
☐ Does the audit assess environmental performance against stated targets?
☐ Does the audit assess the EMS itself?
☐ Is evidence provided to underpin claims of the EMS?
☐ Has an audit report been completed?
☐ Will senior management review the audit?
☐ Has a review report been completed?
☐ Does the review report summarize the main findings of the audit and recommendations arising from it?
☐ Is an action plan produced to follow up review recommendations?

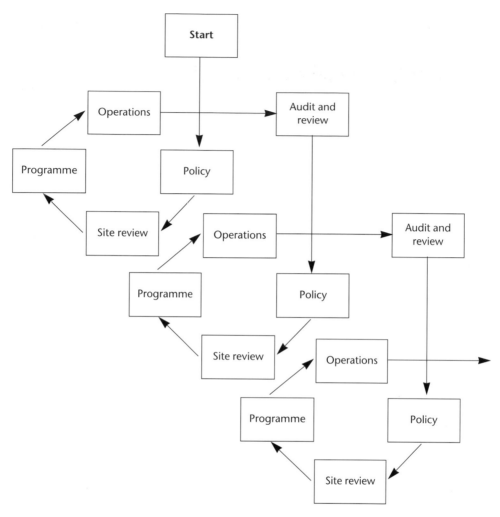

Figure 10.3   Initiation of the next EMS cycle

PART 4

INFORMATION SOURCES

Bibliography

Aldridge, D. (1975) *Guide to Countryside Interpretation: Part One: Principles of Interpretation and Interpretive Planning.* London: HMSO.

Anstey, C., Thompson, S. and Nichols, K. (1982) *Creative Forestry.* Wellington: New Zealand Forest Service.

Barwise, J. (1998) *Environment Management Systems.* Higher Education Funding Council for England (HEFCE).

Beard, C. (1995) Countryside access – a commodity to sell? *Countryside Recreation Network News,* July, 20–3.

Beioley, S. and Denman, R. (1995) *Tourism and the Industrial Heritage of North West England.* London:

Bell, S. (1997) *Design for Outdoor Recreation.* London: E&FN Spon.

Birnie, W. and Boyle, A. (1992) *International Law and the Environment.* Oxford: Oxford University Press.

Bishop, J. (1996) Managing and mediating environmental impact. *Countryside Recreation Network News,* 4(1), 6–8.

Borrini-Feyerabend, G. (1996) *Collaborative Management of Protected Areas: Tailoring the Approach to the Context.* Cambridge: IUCN and The World Conservation Union.

Bramwell, B. (1994) Rural tourism and sustainable tourism. *Journal of Sustainable Tourism,* 2(1/2), 1–6.

British Airways (1996) *Aviation and the Environment.* London: British Airways.

British Airways (1997) *Annual Environmental Report – 1997.* London: British Airways.

British Airways (1998) *Annual Environmental Report – 1998.* London: British Airways.

British Standards Institute (1996) *Environmental Management Systems: Implementation of ISO 14001.* London: British Standards Institute.

Bromley, P. (1994) *Countryside Recreation: A Handbook for Managers.* London: E&FN Spon.

Broom, G. (1991) Environmental management of countryside visitors. *Ecosystem,* 12(1), 14–20.

Brown, A., Vaughan, J. and Gerrard, K. (1993) Sport and recreation in the Community Forests and the National Forest: the Sports Council perspective. *Countryside Recreation Network News,* 3, 9–14.

Brown, P. (1999) More now flee environment than warfare. *The Guardian,* 24 June.

Buckley, R. and Pannell, J. (1990) Environmental impacts of tourism and recreation in national parks and conservation reserves. *Journal of Tourism Studies,* 1(1), 24–32.

Bunin, N., Jasperse, D. and Cooper, S. (1980) *Guide to Designing Accessible Outdoor Recreation Facilities. USDI Heritage Conservation and Recreation Service.* Michigan: Ann Arbor.

Butler, R. (1998) Sustainable tourism – looking backwards in order to progress, in Hall, C. M. and Lew, A. (1998) *Sustainable Tourism: A Geographical Perspective.* Harlow: Longman.

Cater, E. (1995) Environmental contradictions in sustainable tourism. *The Geographical Journal,* 161(1), 21–8.

Ceballous-Lascurain, H. (1996) *Tourism, Ecotourism, and Protected Areas.* Cambridge: International Union for Conservation of Nature and Natural Resources Publications Unit.

Clark, G., Darral, J., Grove-White, R., Macnaghten, P. and Urry, J. (1994) *Leisure Landscapes:*

Leisure, Culture and the English Countryside: Challenges and Conflicts. London: Council for the Protection of Rural England.

Clark, R. N. and Stankey, G. H. (1979) *The Recreation Opportunity Spectrum: A Framework for Planning Management.* Pacific Northwest and Range Experiment Station, Portland, Oregon: USAD Forest Service.

Clayden, P. and Trevelyan, J. (1983) *Rights of Way: A Guide to Law and Practice.* London: Ramblers Association.

Cobham, R. (1990) *Amenity Landscape Management: A Resources Handbook.* London: E&FN Spon.

Cole, D. N. (1994) *The Wilderness Threats Matrix: A Framework for Assessing Impacts.* Ogden, Utah: USAD Forest Service Intermountain Experiment Station.

Collins, B. (2000) Implementing environmental management systems in forest tourism: The case of Center Parcs. In Font, X. and Tribe, J. (eds) (2000) *Forest Tourism and Recreation: Case Studies in Environmental Management.* Wallingford: CAB International.

Commission of the European Communities (1997) *Progress Report and Action Plan on the Fifth Programme of Policy and Action in Relation to the Environment and Sustainable Development.* Luxembourg: Commission of the European Communities.

Commission of the European Union (1994) *Eco-tourism: Culture and Countryside.* Luxembourg: DG XXIII.

Commission of the European Union (1995) *Tourism in Europe.* Luxembourg: Eurostat – DG XXIII.

Council for National Parks (1997) UK Focus: Agenda on transport. *Tourism in Focus,* 25.

Council for the Protection of Rural England (1994) *Leisure Landscapes.* London: Council for the Protection of Rural England.

Countryside Commission (1990) *Green Tourism in the Countryside.* Conference Proceedings April 1990. Cheltenham: Countryside Commission.

Countryside Commission (1991) *Visitors to the Countryside.* CCP 341. Cheltenham: Countryside Commission.

Countryside Commission (1994) *Informal Countryside Recreation for Disabled People: A Practical Guide for Countryside Managers.* Cheltenham: Countryside Commission.

Countryside Commission (1994) *National Forest; The Strategy; The Forest Vision.* Cheltenham: Countryside Commission.

Countryside Commission (1995) *Sustainable Rural Tourism: Opportunities for Local Action Advisory Booklet.* Cheltenham: Countryside Commission.

Countryside Commission, Department of National Heritage, English Tourist Board, Rural Development Commission. (1995) *Sustainable Rural Tourism: Putting it into Practice.* London: Countryside Commission.

Countryside Commission. (1996) *Market Research for Countryside Recreation: A Practical Guide to Market Research for the Providers of Recreation in the Countryside.* Cheltenham: Countryside Commission.

Countryside Recreation Network (1996) *Consensus in the Countryside: Reaching Shared Agreement in Policy, Planning and Management.* Cardiff: Countryside Recreation Network.

Countryside Recreation Network (1996) *UK Day Visits Survey 1994.* Cardiff: Countryside Recreation Network.

Croall, J. (1995) *Preserve or Destroy: Tourism and the Environment.* London: Calouste Gulbenkian Foundation.

Curry, N. R. (1994) *Countryside Recreation, Access and Land Use Planning.* London: E&FN Spon.

Daily, G. and Ehrlich, P. (1992) Population, sustainability and the earth's carrying capacity. *Bioscience,* 42(10), 761–71

Davidson, R. (1998) *Travel and Tourism in Europe,* 2nd edition, Harlow: Longman.

De Clerck, P. and Klingers, J. (1997) The right price for air travel? *Tourism in Focus,* 25.

Deegan, J. and Dineen, D. (1997) *Tourism Policy and Performance.* London: International Thomson Business Press.

Del Nevo, T. (1996) *Wytham Woods Entry Permit.* Oxford University Land Agent.

Denman, R. (1994) Green tourism and farming, in Fladmark, J. (ed.) *Cultural Tourism.* Aberdeen: the Robert Gordon University, 215–22.

Department of the Environment (1994) *Sustainable Development: The UK Strategy.* London: HMSO.

Department of the Environment (1996a) *Indicators of Sustainable Development in the United Kingdom.* London: HMSO.

Department of the Environment (1996b) *EC Eco-management and Audit Scheme: An Introductory Guide for Industry*. London: HMSO.

Department of the Environment (1997a) *EC Eco-management and Audit Scheme: A Participant's Guide*. London: HMSO.

Department of the Environment (1997b) *EC Eco-management and Audit Scheme for UK Local Government*. London: HMSO.

Department of the Environment, Transport and the Regions (1998) *Indicators of Sustainable Development for the United Kingdom*. London: DETR.

Department of the Environment, Transport and the Regions (1998) *The Environment in Your Pocket: Key Facts and Figures on the Environment of the United Kingdom*. Government Statistical Service.

Eden, J. (1996) The Natural Park of Cazorla, Segura and Las Villas: a case study of tourism development in a rural area, in Barke, M., Towner, J. and Newton, M. T. (eds) *Tourism in Spain: Critical Issues*, Wallingford: CABI, 375–400.

Edington, J. M. and Edington, M. A. (1986) *Ecology, Recreation and Tourism*. Cambridge: Press Syndicate.

Elkington, J. and Knight, P. (1992) *The Green Business Guide*. London: Victor Gollancz.

Ellul, A. (1997) Integrating sustainable principles in the development of tourist projects. *Naturopa*, 84(5).

Embacher, H. (1994) Marketing for agri-tourism in Austria: Strategy and realisation in a highly developed tourist destination, in Bramwell, B. and Lane, B. (eds) *Rural Tourism and Sustainable Rural Development*. Clevedon: Channel View Publications, 61–76.

ENDS Report (1999) Aircraft impact on climate to take off. *Environmental Data Services*, 291, 8.

English Nature (1994) *Paintball Games in Woodlands: A Guide to Good Environmental Practice*. London: English Nature:

English Tourist Board (1991) *Tourism and the Environment: Maintaining the Balance*. London: English Tourist Board.

Environment Committee (1995) *The Environmental Impact of Leisure Activities*. Vol. 1. London: HMSO.

Fisher, R. J. (1995) *Collaborative Management of Forests for Conservation and Development*. Cambridge: IUCN and The World Conservation Union.

FNNPE (The Federation of Nature and National Parks of Europe) (1993) *Loving Them to Death? The Need for Sustainable Tourism in Europe's Nature and National Parks*. Grafenau, Germany: FNNPE.

Font, X. and Tribe, J. (2000) Recreation, conservation and timber production: a sustainable relationship?, in Font, X. and Tribe, J. (eds) (2000) *Forest Tourism and Recreation: Case Studies in Environmental Management*. Wallingford: CAB International.

Forest Authority (1998) *The UK Forestry Standard*. Edinburgh: Forestry Commission.

Forestry Commission (1990a) *Forest Nature Conservation Guidelines*. Edinburgh: Forestry Commission.

Forestry Commission (1990b) *Recofax: Recreation Planning, Design and Management Information Sheets*. Edinburgh: Forestry Commission.

Forestry Commission (1992a) *Community Woodland Design: Guidelines*. Edinburgh: Forestry Commission.

Forestry Commission (1992b) *Forest Recreation: Guidelines*. London: HMSO.

Forestry Commission (1994a) *Forest Landscape Design: Guidelines*. Edinburgh: Forestry Commission.

Forestry Commission (1994b) *Reports on Forest Research*. Edinburgh: Forestry Commission.

FSC (Forest Stewardship Council) (1994) *Forest Stewardship Principles and Criteria for Natural Forest Management*. Oaxaca, Mexico: FSC.

Gannon, A. (1994) Rural tourism as a factor in rural community economic development for economies in transition. *Journal of Sustainable Tourism*, 2(1/2), 51–60.

Gilbert, J. (1993) *Achieving Environmental Management Standards: A Step-by-step Guide to Meeting BS7750*. London: Pitman.

Gilg, A. (1996) *Countryside Planning*, 2nd edition. London: Routledge.

Glypsis, S. (1991) *Countryside Recreation*. London: Longman.

Goodall, B. and Whittow, J. B. (1975) Recreational requirements and forest opportunities. *Geographical Papers* No. 37. Reading: University of Reading.

Grayson, L. (1992) *BS 7750: What the New Environmental Management Standard Means for your Business*. Hertfordshire: Technical Communications.

Green Globe (1999) *Green Globe 21 Standards*. Cambridge: Green Globe.

Green, B. (1981) *Countryside Conservation*. London: Allen and Unwin.

Gunn, C. (1994) *Tourism Planning*, 3rd edition. London: Taylor and Francis.

Haigh, N. (1992) *Manual of Environmental Policy: The EC and Britain*. Harlow: Longman.

Hall, D. and O'Hanlon, L. (eds) (1998) *Rural Tourism Management: Sustainable Options*, Conference proceedings. Ayr, Scotland: Scottish Agricultural College.

Ham, S. H. (1992) *Environmental Interpretation: A Practical Guide for People with Big Ideas and Small Budgets*. Colorado: North American Press.

Harmon, D. (ed.) (1994) *Co-ordinating Research and Management to Enhance Protected Areas*. Cambridge: IUCN and The World Conservation Union.

Haukeland, J. V. (1998) Foreign tourists' interests in accommodation in cabins for hire as an option for tourism development in rural areas, in Hall, D. and O'Halon, L. (eds) *Rural Tourism Management: Sustainable Options*, Conference proceedings, Ayr, Scotland: Scottish Agricultural College.

Hawkes, P. and Williams, P. (1993) *The Greening of Tourism, From Principles to Practice: A Case of Best Environmental Practice in Tourism*. Canada: Simon Fraser University.

Herbert, D. T. (1989) *Heritage Sites: Strategies for Marketing and Development*. Aldershot: Avebury.

Henson, L. (1990) The US Forest Service recreation strategy: bringing the great outdoors to the American people, in Hilary Talbot (ed.) *People, Trees and Woods: Proceedings of the 1989 Countryside Recreation Conference*, 7–14.

Hillary, R. (ed.) (1997) *Environmental Management Systems and Cleaner Production*. Chichester: Wiley.

HMSO (Her Majesty's Stationery Office) (1990) *This Common Inheritance*. White Paper. London: HMSO.

HMSO (Her Majesty's Stationery Office) (1992) *Sustainable Development: The UK Strategy*. London: HMSO.

Hummel, F. C. (1992) Aspects of forest recreation in Western Europe. *Forestry*, 65(3), 237–51.

Hunter, C. and Green, H. (1995) *Tourism and the Environment: a Sustainable Relationship?* London: Routledge.

ILAM (Institute of Leisure and Amenity Management) (1998) *Management Systems for Best Value. Fact sheet 98/2*. Reading: ILAM Information Centre.

International Hotels Environment Initiative (1994) *Environmental Management for Hotels: The Industry Guide to Best Practice*. Oxford: Butterworth Heinemann.

Irving, J. A. (1985) *The Public in Your Woods*. Chichester: Packard.

IUCN (The World Conservation Union) (1995) *Best Practice for Conservation Planning in Rural Areas*. Gland, Switzerland: IUCN.

Jackson, J. (1997) Hanging out in the woods. *Quarterly Journal of Forestry*, 91(2), 60–2.

Jim, C. H. (1989) Visitor Management in Recreation Areas. *Environmental Conservation*, 16(1), 19–32.

Kirk, D. (1997) *Environmental Management for Hotels: A Student's Handbook*. Oxford: Butterworth-Heinemann.

Kiss, A. and Shelton, D. (1997) *Manual of European Environmental Law*. Cambridge: Cambridge University Press.

Koeig, K. M. and Headley, J. (1995) Sustainable forest management, where do you fit in? *Wood and Wood Products*, 100, 43–7.

Lane, B. (1994) What is rural tourism? *Journal of Sustainable Tourism*, 2(1/2), 7–21.

Lascelles, D. (1995) The country: for work, rest or play? – The battle for control of rural Britain is hotting up. *Financial Times*, 14 October.

Lee, T. (1990) What kind of woodland and forest do people prefer? in Hilary Talbot (ed.) *People, Trees and Woods: Proceedings of the 1989 Countryside Recreation Conference*, 37–52.

Leu, W. (1996) Le produit suisse du tourisme rural, in WTO, *Rural Tourism: A Solution for Employment, Local Development and Environment*. Madrid: WTO.

Levy, G. M. (1993) *Packaging and the Environment*. London: Blackie.

Local Government Management Board (1995a) *EMAS Help-desk Guidance Notes: Undertaking an Environmental Review*. London: Local Government Management Board.

Local Government Management Board (1995b) *EMAS Help-desk Guidance Notes: Writing an Environmental Policy.* London: Local Government Management Board.

Local Government Management Board (1995c) *EMAS Help-desk Guidance Notes: Writing an Environmental Programme.* London: Local Government Management Board.

Local Government Management Board (1996a) *EMAS Help-desk Guidance Notes: Writing an Environmental Policy: Update.* London: Local Government Management Board.

Local Government Management Board (1996b) *EMAS Help-desk Guidance Notes: A Guide to the Management System and Audit Stages of EMAS for UK Local Government.* London: Local Government Management Board.

Local Government Management Board (1996c) *EMAS Help-desk Guidance Notes. Environmental Effects Evaluation (EEE).* London: Local Government Management Board.

Mathieson, A. and Wall, G. (1982) *Tourism: Economic, Physical and Social Impacts.* Harlow: Longman.

McGowan, K. (1996) Mountain biking: perceptual problem, passing fad or positive management? *Countryside Recreation Network News*, 4(1), 12–13.

McIntyre, E. and Hetherington, A. (1991) *Sustainable Tourism Development. Guidelines for Local Planners.* Madrid: WTO.

McKercher, B. (1996) Differences between tourism and recreation in parks. *Annals of Tourism Research*, 23(3), 563–75.

Ministry of Agriculture, Fisheries and Food (1995) *Balance in the Countryside: Information Pack.* London: Ministry of Agriculture, Fisheries and Food.

Mintel (1996) *Sporting Activities in the 'Great Outdoors'.* London: Mintel.

Mintel (1998) *Special Interest Holidays, Leisure Intelligence.* London: Mintel.

Murphey, D. and Bendell, J. (1997) *In the Company of Partners.* London: The Policy Press.

National Park Commission (1978) *The Country Code.* Reviewed from the National Parks and Access to the Countryside Act (1949).

Nelson, J. G., Butler, R. and Wall, G. (1993) *Tourism and Sustainable Development: Monitoring, Planning, Managing.* Waterloo: University of Waterloo.

OECD (1975) *The Polluter Pays Principle: Definition, Analysis, Implementation.* Paris: OECD

OECD (1990) *Bergen Ministerial Declaration on Sustainable Development.* Bergen: OECD.

Page, S. and Getz, D. (1997) The business of rural tourism: international perspectives, in Page, S. and Getz, D. (eds) *The Business of Rural Tourism: International Perspectives*, London: International Thomson Business Press, 3–37.

Pearce, D., Markandya, A. and Barbier, E. (1989) *Blueprint for a Green Economy.* London: Earthscan.

Perera, O. (1997) Cleaner production in tourism: From theory to practice. *Naturopa*, 84, 12–13.

Plimmer, N. (1994) Everyone benefits? The case of New Zealand. *Environment and Development Report.* London: WTTC.

Priestley, G., Edwards, J., and Coccossis, H. (1996) *Sustainable Tourism? European Experiences.* Wallingford: CAB International.

Pritchard, P. C. (1992) *Carrying Capacity for Protected Areas: An Overview.* Paper presented at the IV World Congress on National Parks and Protected Areas.

Responsible Forestry Programme (1994) *Responsible Forestry Standards.* Bristol: The Soil Association Marketing Company Ltd.

Roberts, G. (1996) How many more can we take? Assessing recreational capacity. *Countryside Recreation Network News*, 4(1), 4–5.

Rogers, H. A and Slinn, J. A. (1993) *Tourism: Management of Facilities.* London: Pitman.

Royal Institution of Chartered Surveyors/Royal Town Planning Institute (1993) *Tomorrow's Countryside: Management, Conservation and Enjoyment: A Policy Initiative.* London: Royal Institution of Chartered Surveyors.

Russell, D. (2000) Managing compatibility of recreation and forestry, in Font, X. and Tribe, J. (eds) (2000) *Forest Tourism and Recreation: Case Studies in Environmental Management.* Wallingford: CAB International.

Selman, P. (1992) *Environmental Planning: The Conservation and Development of Biophysical Resources.* London: Paul Chapman Publishing.

Sharpley, R. (1996) *Tourism and Leisure in the Countryside* (2nd edition). Huntingdon: ELM.

Sharpley, R. and Sharpley, J. (1997) *Rural Tourism: An Introduction.* London: International Thomson Business Press.

Sheldon, C. (1996) First steps on the thousand-mile journey: a brief overview of the ISO 14000 series of standards. *Environmental Policy and Practice*, 6(3), 125–30.

Soil Association (1994) *Responsible Forestry Programme: Responsible Forestry Standards*. Bristol: The Soil Association.

Tarasofsky, R. G. (1995) *The International Forest Regime: Legal and Policy Issues*. Cambridge: IUCN and The World Conservation Union.

The Earthworks Group (1995) *Earth Limited: 50 Simple Things Your Business Can Do to Save the Earth*. Leeds: Essential Public Relations.

The Rural Development Commission (1996) *The Green Audit Kit: A DIY Guide to Greening Your Tourism Business*. Bristol: The Rural Development Commission.

Tilden, F. (1957) *Interpreting Our Heritage*. London: Chapel Hill.

Todd, S. and Williams, P. (1996) From white to green: a proposed environmental management system framework for ski areas. *Journal of Sustainable Tourism*, Vol. 4(3), 147–73.

Tomkins, J. (1990) Recreation and the Forestry Commission: the case for multiple-use resource management within public forestry in the UK. *Journal of Environmental Management*, 30(1) 79–88.

TQM International Ltd (1996) *Support for Continuous Improvement: Performance Measurement Workbook*. Cheshire: TQM International Ltd.

Transport 2000 (1989) *No Through Road*. UK: Transport 2000.

Tribe, J. (1998) Tourfor: an environmental management systems approach to tourism and recreation in forest areas, in Hall, D. and O'Hanlon, L., *Rural Tourism Management: Sustainable Options*. Scotland: International Conference Proceedings Scottish Agricultural College, 561–77.

UNEP (United Nations Environment Programme) Industry and Environment (1995) *Technical Report 29. Environmental Codes of Conduct for Tourism*.

UNEP (United Nations Environment Programme) Industry and Environment (1998) *Ecolabels in the Tourism Industry*. Paris: UNEP.

Valentine, P. S. (1991) Eco-tourism and nature tourism/conservation. A definition with recent developments. *Tourism Management*, 14(2), 107–15.

Vickery, R. (1998) Non-consumptive wildlife-orientated recreation: conflict, coexistence or symbiosis, in Hall, D. and O'Hanlon, L. *Rural Tourism Management: Sustainable Options*. Scotland: International Conference Proceedings Scottish Agricultural College, 597–613.

Walters, G., Angell, B., Mayes, D. and Wingate, P. (1994) Training for the management of countryside recreation. *Countryside Recreation Network News*, 2(2), 1–2, 8–13.

Wight, P. (1998) Tools for sustainability analysis in planning and managing tourism and recreation in the destination, in Hall, C. M. and Lew, A. (1998) *Sustainable Tourism: A Geographical Perspective*. Harlow: Longman.

Williams, A. and Shaw, G. (eds) (1988) *Tourism and Economic Development: West European Experiences*. London: Belhaven Press.

Williams, A. M. and Shaw, G. (eds) (1996) *Tourism, Leisure, Nature Protection and Agri-tourism: Principles, Partnerships and Practice*. Exeter: European Partners for the Environment. Tourism Research Group.

Williams, R. (1975) *The Country and the City*. London: Paladin.

Willis, K. G. and Garrod, G. D. (1991) An individual travel–cost method of evaluating forest recreation. *Journal of Agricultural Economics*, 42(1), 33–42.

Woodward, D. (1994) Is going green cost effective? *Voice*, 18 September.

World Commission on Environment and Development (1987) *Our Common Future*. Oxford: Oxford University Press.

World Tourism Organization (1996) *Rural Tourism: A Solution for Employment, Local Development and Environment*. Madrid: WTO.

World Travel and Tourism Council, World Tourism Organization and Earth Council (1995) *Agenda 21 for the Travel and Tourism Industry: Towards Environmentally Sustainable Development*.

World Travel and Tourism Environment Research Centre (1993) *World Travel and Tourism Environment Review – 1993: Environment and Development*. WTTC.

Worpole, K. (1999) Driving forces. *The Guardian*, 8 June.

Yarrow, A. (ed) (1998) *Exploring Woodlands in the South East*. Reading: Forestry Trust for Conservation and Education.

Glossary

Abnormal event An unusual or irregular occurrence, but an expected one; for example, a Bank Holiday or special event.

Accreditation The examination of the competence of a certifying body, and the granting of certifying powers.

Activities All leisure pursuits and management aspects carried out on a site.

Agenda 21 One of the five documents agreed upon at the United Nations Conference on Environment and Development (UNCED), in Rio de Janeiro in June 1992. Signed by 179 heads of government, it is the blueprint for sustainable development in the twenty-first century, aimed at providing a high-quality environment and healthy economy for all the peoples of the world.

Alien species Plant or animal species introduced from elsewhere and naturalized in a region.

Amenity A site facility, e.g. visitor centre.

Audit A check to assess the performance of an EMS.

Baseline The starting point.

Conservation The planning and management of resources so as to secure their wide use and continuity of supply, while maintaining and possibly enhancing their quality, value and diversity.

Consumption of resources To use up a stock or supply of anything that can be used to provide the means to satisfy human needs and wants.

Coppicing Cutting shrubs or trees close to the ground to allow new shoots to grow from the stumps or stools, on a rotational basis.

Cost–benefit analysis Comparison of the costs of an action against the benefits generated.

Countryside Rural parts of the country.

Defined Forest Area A forest area where the exact boundaries can be physically identified.

Demography The study of the population.

Disseminate To spread information.

Destination The place to which one is going.

Development Change of land use from forestry or agriculture for building and urbanization.

Disturbance Any event that alters the structure, composition, or functions of an ecosystem.

Ecosystem The plants and animals that live in a defined space, which can range from a desert to an ocean, and the physical environment in which they live comprise together an ecosystem.

Emergency event An unexpected event that is out of the ordinary, for example a pollution incident or fire.

Energy The means of doing work. Energy has many forms: electrical, chemical, mechanical, nuclear, heat, light and sound.

Environment All of the surroundings including living things, climate and physical features.

Environmental impact An impingement on the environment.

Environmental target A clear and achievable objective for environmental improvement

EMS Environmental Management System.

Environmental Management System (EMS) A systematic structure of an organization's internal configuration specifically designed to control and monitor environmental interactions.

Environmental Management System (EMS) Manual Used to store the documentation associated with an EMS.

Erosion The wearing away of the earth's surface by weathering, corrosion and transportation, under the influence of gravity, wind and running water.

Facility Anything specially arranged or constructed in this context to support recreation or leisure.

Finite Limited, bounded and of fixed quantity.

Forest A large tract of land covered with trees and underwood.

Forestry The act of planting, tending and managing predominantly tree-covered land (woodland) whether in large tracts (generally called forests) or smaller units (known by a variety of terms such as woods, copses and shelterbeds).

Guidelines An indication of a course to follow.

Habitat and species loss The loss of the natural home of an animal or a plant.

Habitat change The alteration or modification to the natural home of an animal or plant.

Leisure The time remaining after working, commuting, sleeping, and doing necessary household and personal chores which can be used in a chosen way.

Management action Work undertaken in this context to alleviate an environmental impact.

Measuring A way of quantifying the extent of environmental impacts.

Monitoring The continued measurement, and evaluation of environmental impacts to ascertain an organization's environmental performance against agreed environmental targets.

Mulch Material laid down on the soil surface to protect plant roots and discourage weed growth.

Omission To leave something out.

Operations Implementation of the environmental programme.

Policy Statement of the overall environmental aims of a site and its management.

Pollard A tree having being cut at 2–4 metres above ground level, leaving it to send out new branches from the top of the exposed stem.

Pollution The introduction into the environment of substances or impacts that are potentially harmful or interfere with mankind's use of the environment or interfere with species or habitats.

Prioritization Giving precedence in rank or order of management to one significant impact over another.

Procedure A mode of conducting a series of actions in a certain order or manner. Describes who will take what action, how the action will be taken and where the action will be taken.

Programme The formal agenda for action.

Project A scheme of something to be done.

Qualitative Analysis by words.

Quantitative Analysis by figures.

Recreation Activities undertaken in leisure time.

Review Closes the loop of the EMS by assessing the information collected in the audit to decide upon corrective action.

Rural Of the country, non-urban.

Scheduling Establishing a timetable that plans and arranges management tasks to happen at a specified time.

Sequencing To place management tasks in the order that they will be completed.

Service The act or mode of serving. Providing services rather than manufactured goods.

Significant impact Of considerable importance and possible influence.

Site review An assessment of a site and an organization's current environmental management status.

Site The area of land that an organization operates within.

Stakeholder A person or grouping with an interest in the operation of a particular organization.

Standard An expected level of quality, graded against competitors/similar industry or a theoretical classification.

Sustainability Development that meets the needs of the present generation without compromising the ability of future generations to meet their own needs

Task A piece or amount of the work undertaken through a management action.

Topography The detailed features of the land.

Tourism A temporary movement to a destination outside the normal home and workplace for at least one night for leisure and holiday, business and professional or other tourism purposes

Tourism attraction A designated permanent resource, which is controlled and managed for the enjoyment, amusement, entertainment, and education of the visiting public.

Trampling The action of pressing down with feet, crushing, and treating roughly or even with contempt.

UNCED United Nations Conference on Environment and Development

Vegetation loss The disappearance, perishment, loss or death of plants and plant life collectively.

Verifier The person licensed to evaluate the claims of a site.

Visitor A person who visits, calls on, or makes a stay to a tourism attraction.

Waste Any matter, whether liquid, solid, gaseous, or radioactive, which is discharged, emitted, or deposited in the environment in such volume, concentration, constituency, or manner as to cause a significant alteration of the environment.

WTTC World Travel and Tourism Council.

Useful Addresses

Environment

British Trust for Conservation Volunteers
BTCV is the UK's largest practical conservation organization. It works with and provides advice to landowners, local authorities, business, community groups and individuals.

> BTCV
> 36 St Mary's Street
> Wallingford
> Oxon OX10 0EU
> Tel: 01491 839766; Fax: 01491 839646
> www.btcv.org

Countryside Agency
The Countryside Agency works to conserve and enhance the countryside and promotes social equity and economic opportunity for the people who live and work in rural areas. This is achieved through research and advice, grant schemes and practical projects.

> Countryside Agency
> John Dower House
> Crescent Place
> Cheltenham
> Gloucestershire GL50 3RA
> Tel: 01242 521381; Fax: 01242 584270
> www.countryside.gov.uk

Department of the Environment for Northern Ireland
The DoENI acts as the agent for DETR in the administration in Northern Ireland of UK-wide schemes.

> DoENI
> Environment and Heritage Service
> Calvert House
> 23 Castle Place
> Belfast, Northern Ireland
> Tel: 028 9025 4754; Fax: 028 9025 4700
> www.doeni.gov.uk/index.htm

Department for the Environment, Transport and the Regions
DETR is the government department for the UK which develops policy, and advises on many different areas, including planning, rural development, water, waste and air quality and legislation.

> DETR
> Eland House
> Bressenden Place
> London SW1E 5DU
> Tel: 020 7890 3000
> www.detr.gov.uk

English Nature
English Nature is the statutory body which achieves, enables and promotes nature conservation in England.

> English Nature
> Northminster House
> Peterborough PE1 1UA
> Tel: 01733 455000; Fax: 01733 68834
> www.english-nature.gov.uk

Environment Agency
The Environment Agency is a non-departmental public body and is responsible for water resources and pollution control and enforcing environmental law.

> Environment Agency
> Rio House
> Waterside Drive
> Aztec West
> Almondsbury
> Bristol BS12 4UD
> Tel: 01454 624400;Fax: 01454 624409
> www.environment-agency.gov.uk

Forestry Commission
This includes the Forestry Authority and

Forest Enterprise. It is the government department responsible for forestry in Great Britain. It sets the standards for the forestry industry, and provides information, advice and grants for forestry operations.

Forestry Commission
231 Corstophine Road
Edinburgh EH12 7AT
Tel: 0131 334 0303; Fax: 0131 334 3047
www.forestry.gov.uk

Farming and Wildlife Advisory Group
FWAG provides a conservation advisory service to farmers and landowners, and offers information on grant schemes.

FWAG
National Agricultural Centre
Stoneleigh
Kenilworth
Warwickshire CV8 2RX
Tel: 024 7669 6699; Fax: 024 7669 6760
www.snw.org.uk/enweb/fwag.htm

Scottish Office Agriculture, Environment and Fisheries Department
SOAEFD implements government policy for agricultural, environmental and fishery schemes in Scotland, and provides an advisory service.

SOAEFD
Pentland House
47 Robbs Loan
Edinburgh EH14 1TW
Tel: 0131 556 8400; Fax: 0131 244 4071

Management

European Commission
The EC has representation in each member state for the purpose of assisting the EC to implement its duties and to pursue its information and communication policy.

The European Commission
8 Storey's Gate
London SW1P 3AT
Tel: 020 7973 1992; Fax: 020 7973 1910
www.cec.org.uk/index.htm

British Standards Institution
A recognized quality assurance organization. It is the independent national body responsible for preparing British standards. It presents the UK view on International and European standards and provides a wide range of information on standards

BSI
389 Chiswick High Road

London W4 4AL
Tel: 020 8996 9000; Fax: 020 8996 7400

Tourism

Department for Culture, Media and Sport
The tourism division within this government department is responsible for tourism policy in England and for promoting tourism to Great Britain.

Department for Culture, Media and Sport.
Tourism Division
2–4 Cockspur Street
London SW1Y 5DH
Tel: 020 7211 6328; Fax: 020 7211 6319
www.culture.gov.uk/index.html

The Tourist Boards
The tourist boards are statutory bodies with the aim of encouraging the provision and improvement of tourist amenities in the UK and developing the market in ways which yield economic and social benefit to local people.

English Tourist Board
Thames Tower
Blacks Road
London W6 9EL
Tel: 020 8846 9000; Fax: 020 8563 0302
www.etb.org.uk

Scottish Tourist Board
23 Ravelston Terrace
Edinbourgh EH4 3EU
Tel: 0131 332 2433; Fax: 0131 343 1513
www.holiday.scotland.net/

Welsh Tourist Board
Press Office, Brunel House,
2 Fitzalan Rd,
Cardiff CF2 1UY
Tel: 029 2047 5272; Fax: 029 2047 5322
www.tourism.wales.gov.uk

World Travel and Tourism Council
The WTTC is the global business leader's forum for travel and tourism. Its central goal is to work with governments to realize the full economic impacts of this industry.

WTTC
20 Grosvernor Place
London SW1X 7TT
Tel: 020 7838 9400; Fax: 020 7838 9050
www.wttc.org

Index